POLICY
G U I D E

FOR WASHINGTON STATE

6th Edition
Edited by Paul Guppy

POLICY
G U I D E
FOR WASHINGTON STATE

Table of Contents

POLICY
G U I D E
FOR WASHINGTON STATE

Foreword
by Daniel Mead Smith, President

Thank you for your interest in this 6th edition of the Policy Guide for Washington State and our work at Washington Policy Center (WPC). We are an independent, non-profit research and educational organization with offices in Seattle, Olympia, Spokane and the Tri-Cities.

The majority of our supporters are individuals, families and small business owners. Over 90 percent of our support comes from in-state sources. All contributions are independent and voluntary; we do not receive government money.

Our research program is centered on eight areas of public policy: budget, taxes and government reform; protecting the environment; promoting agriculture; reforming health care; improving education; protecting small business; improving transportation; and promoting labor reform and worker rights. We also provide a free, nonpartisan website, WashingtonVotes.org, to inform people about bills, roll call votes and other legislative action taking place at the state capitol.

We use many sources in our research, particularly data and reports provided by local, state and federal government agencies. However, all findings, conclusions and policy recommendations are determined solely by WPC analysts, based on objective and well-sourced research.

Typical users of our research are state lawmakers, agency officials, city and county officials, reporters for print, broadcast and online media and our thousands of members across the state. News organizations frequently use WPC research when covering public issues. Our experts and research findings and policy recommendations are cited in news reports over a thousand times every year.

Washington Policy Center is not a political organization. We promote ideas and independent research, not parties or candidates. Our experts serve as a resource to lawmakers of both parties to promote sound policies that benefit the people of Washington.

Similar to the 5th edition of our Policy Guide, this new edition presents what we believe are the best ideas and reforms needed to make the greatest positive difference for the people of our great state. These are the policy recommendations that we think policymakers should adopt as their main priorities.

We hope you find this latest edition of the Policy Guide for Washington State both useful and informative. Its purpose is to advance better governance and policy reforms that benefit the people of our state. As such, it is a key part of the mission of Washington Policy Center, which is to promote public policy ideas that improve the lives of all Washingtonians. You can learn more at www.washingtonpolicy.org.

POLICY
G U I D E
FOR WASHINGTON STATE

Introduction to the 6th Edition
by Paul Guppy, Vice President for Research

This 6th edition of the Policy Guide for Washington State has been revised and updated with the latest research to provide elected officials and the general public with sound ideas that benefit all people living in in our state.

Policy ideas based on solid data and which enhance freedom and opportunity allow individuals, families and communities to make decisions for themselves without interfering with the rights of others, while providing safety-net services for those most in need.

Chapter 1 provides ways to control the growth in public spending so it meets the legitimate needs of government, rather than simply spending the maximum elected officials can get in taxes. Each year state spending increases faster than the natural rise in inflation and population, showing that officials routinely take more money from working families and business owners than they really need.

Chapter 2 recommends that lawmakers provide the people with tax relief. By lightening the financial burden they impose, elected leaders can show they understand the concerns of working families. Tax relief increases take-home pay for everyone and shows respect for the dignity of workers. In particular, reducing broad-based taxation like sales and property rates allows most of the benefit to go to low-income households.

Chapter 3 shows how new technology and individual action can do more to protect the environment than aggressive top-down programs. Harsh environmental rules impose huge costs on communities and business owners but often do little to solve real-world problems. This Policy Guide shows how people responding to voluntary incentives in their daily lives can do more for the planet than massive government programs.

Chapter 4 provides practical ideas for expanding individual and family access to affordable health care. The core principle is to put patients in charge of their own health care dollars, rather than forcing people into public entitlement programs. Repealing mandates and legal bans on how patients can buy affordable coverage results in lower costs and wider choices in receiving medical care.

Chapter 5 presents data that promotes family choice in education, whether through public charter schools, tax-credit scholarships, family-based vouchers or online learning. In all these cases key decisions about education are made by parents, who can direct public resources in ways that best serve children, instead of simply adding money to the local school district monopoly.

Chapter 6 recommends constructive ways state leaders can re-build public trust in government. Over time the legislature and state agencies have become hide-bound and insensitive, as special interests push their own agendas at the expense of the needs of the public. Greater openness and honesty in how state leaders conduct the people's business would help restore people's faith in their public servants.

Chapters 7 and 8 provide sound recommendations for promoting job-creation and economic growth. These ideas are not simply about making money, they are intended to help state leaders show respect for the life choices of citizens. Widening the sphere of private action allows people to plan, build and succeed for themselves, demonstrating that government exists to serve them – not the other way around.

Chapter 9 provides practical ideas for increasing mobility and freedom of movement. Many elected leaders insist on trying to "force people out of their cars," while the vast majority of the public simply want affordable, flexible and efficient transportation. There is always a role for public transit, but research in this chapter shows how state leaders can deliver on what they routinely promise; congestion relief and public roads that are free-flowing and open to all.

Finally, Chapter 10 shows how state leaders can be responsive to the needs of farmers and rural communities. This is not just a matter of recognizing another economic interest. Agriculture is a way of life, one that is essential to defeating hunger and providing food security for everyone. Agricultural production contributes to the health of the entire state, and to that of people living in national and world markets that benefit from the produce of Washington farms and ranches.

As these brief summaries show, the theme of the <u>Policy Guide for Washington State</u> is to promote growth, opportunity and self-reliance. Powerful forces in our state seek to increase the control of government over our lives, collect more money through high taxation, and funnel money to entrenched interests that profit from public spending.

The purpose of this book is to help policymakers resist this trend, by providing over three dozen independent, non-partisan and unbiased policy recommendations, backed by objective research, that benefit all families and communities in our state.

By adopting these fact-based ideas, state leaders can provide effective public services that allow people to organize their lives, families and communities as they think best, so everyone can thrive within a governing system based on individual rights, mutual respect and ordered liberty.

Introduction

CHAPTER ONE
RESPONSIBLE PUBLIC SPENDING

1. Policy Recommendation: Adopt improved budget transparency to inform the public about spending decisions

The state's combined budgets (operating, capital and transportation) run to hundreds of pages and spend billions in taxpayer dollars. Lawmakers and the Governor tax this money away from the people of Washington and collect it in the treasury. Then they are supposed to spend it for the public's benefit.

Yet despite the length and complexity of these documents, public hearings are usually held the same day the budgets are introduced, and they are then amended and enacted without enough time for meaningful public input. Often the Governor signs budget bills quickly without receiving considered input from the public.

Allowing genuine detailed review by the public before legislative hearings or votes on budget bills would increase public trust in government and would enhance lawmakers' accountability for the spending decisions they make.

At a minimum, the time provided before the legislature holds a public hearing or votes on a budget bill should be 24 hours after full details of the proposal are made public. One day is not too much to ask for public accountability. Ideally, lawmakers should provide even more time for public review.

Make budget offers public

As for budget negotiations between the House and Senate, the spending proposals that are exchanged privately between members of the House and Senate should be made publicly available. Lawmakers may say that they cannot negotiate the budget in public (even though local government officials do just that). There is no reason, however, that the proposals of each side cannot be publicly posted before secret budget meetings are held so that everyone can see what is being proposed and what compromises are being included in the final budget deal.

Not only would the public have a better idea of what is occurring with the state's most important legislation, but lawmakers would also know what positions legislative leadership recommended, so there would be no surprises when final roll call votes are taken.

Enact needed policy changes before a budget vote

Another budget reform would be to prohibit a vote on the operating budget until all the policies necessary to carry out a balanced budget have been passed first. By actually voting on the policy changes, like tax increases, necessary to balance a proposed budget, the House and Senate would know exactly what level of funding would be under each budget proposal, and that each house can actually muster the votes necessary to implement the budget its members are proposing.

2. Policy Recommendation: Place performance outcomes in the budget to hold public agencies accountable

As holders of the state's purse strings, lawmakers are in the best position to pose the "Why" question to be answered by agencies before authorizing taxpayer dollars to be spent. One way to accomplish this is for the legislature to require agency managers to identify at least one expected performance outcome for each program they are seeking to fund.

This process would become the legislature's version of budget instructions to agencies. This would re-focus state budget hearings on whether public programs are actually working and whether they should continue to exist. Public programs often fail, and lawmakers should have an equitable measure of what works and what does not work, rather than blindly funding government programs every year simply because they already exist.

To improve budget accountability, high-level performance expectations should be written directly into the budget, so lawmakers and citizens can quickly see whether policy goals have been met, before agency requests for new or increased spending are approved.

3. Policy Recommendation: Adopt budget reforms to end the threat of a government shutdown

During recent budget cycles, Washington lawmakers have come dangerously close to forcing a government shutdown due to failures in the budget process. The 2017-19 state budget was signed just after 11:00 p.m. on the last day of the funding period, barely beating the midnight deadline. The 2015-17 state budget was signed just 18 minutes before a government shutdown would have occurred. The 2013-15 budget was finalized just a few hours before state agencies would have been forced to close. Such reckless irresponsibility would get private-sector managers fired.

In each case, the tax revenue paid by citizens had increased substantially, meaning threatened government shutdowns were occurring during times of rising revenues, not deficits. The government has plenty of money, lawmakers and the Governor simply cannot agree on how to spend it.

Describing the problem this type of secret-budget-brinksmanship creates, former state Senator Guy Palumbo said in 2017:[1]

"This year's budget process has been a nightmare. With the threat of a government shutdown mere hours away, we produced and passed an operating budget without any public input.

"Not to mention, most legislators, myself included, were given only a few hours to review the budget – a document that is 620 pages long. This is unacceptable, especially when we are implementing monumental K-12 education reform that will have an impact for generations to come."

Three ways to prevent a government shutdown

There is no reason a government shutdown should occur, even in a deficit situation, let alone at a time of rising tax revenues. To end this threat, lawmakers should enact reforms that assure people who rely on vital government services that a political impasse will not close agency doors.

Here are three structural reforms lawmakers should adopt:

1. Early-action base budget at the beginning of the legislative session (as in Utah);

2. Continuing resolution enactment in the last week of a regular session if no budget is passed (as in New Hampshire, North Carolina and South Carolina);

3. Constitutional amendment authorizing continuing appropriations at current spending levels if there is no budget by the end of the session (as in Rhode Island and Wisconsin).

---

1 "2017-19 budget: "This deal is getting worse all the time," by Jason Mercier, Washington Policy Center, July 8, 2017, at https://www.washingtonpolicy.org/publications/detail/2017-19-budget-this-deal-is-getting-worse-all-the-time.

Under an early action base budget process, budget writers from the state House and Senate would meet on a day between the November revenue forecast and the beginning of the legislative session in January to agree on a base budget framework.

This would ensure that current spending levels could be maintained under projected revenue. Then lawmakers would review and approve the base budget during the first weeks of the legislative session so state government operations would continue at current spending levels in case a budget impasse occurs late in the session.

Giving lawmakers time to consider the "real" budget

After approval of a contingency base budget, the rest of the legislative session would be devoted to debating whether lawmakers should increase or decrease the "real" budget compared to the base budget levels to reflect the updated revenue numbers provided by the February state revenue forecast.

Another option lawmakers should consider is to enact a continuing resolution during the last week of session when no formal budget agreement has been reached. This is similar to the base budget process used in Utah, but action happens at the end of session instead of at the beginning. States that use this budget fail-safe process include New Hampshire, North Carolina and South Carolina.

The early-action base budget and continuing resolution safeguards require the legislature to take positive action to avoid a government shutdown. Though the hope is that lawmakers would do so, there is no guarantee they would act in time. This is why the automatic continuation of spending at current levels, a policy used by Rhode Island and Wisconsin, should be considered.

Article 8, Section 4 of the Washington state constitution requires the legislature to approve all appropriations before public money can be spent, so adopting a policy that automatically continues spending at current levels into a new fiscal year would likely require voters to pass a constitutional amendment.

Assuring the public

Adoption of one of these three proven budget reforms — using a base budget process, approval of a continuing resolution, or authorizing continued spending at current levels until a budget can be adopted — would end the threat of a government shutdown in our state.

Ideally, lawmakers should come to a budget agreement during the 105-day regular legislative session. But as history has continually demonstrated, the public cannot be assured of that happy outcome. That is why structural budget reforms are needed to prevent the doubt and uncertainty created by threatened state government shutdowns, and to assure the public that essential programs will continue.

4. Policy Recommendation: Restore legislative oversight of collective bargaining agreements

In 2002 Governor Gary Locke signed a bill, HB 1268, that fundamentally altered the balance of power between the Governor and legislature concerning state employee pay and benefits in the budget. The bill's purpose was to reform Washington's civil service laws and for the first time in state history, give state employee union executives the power to negotiate directly with the Governor behind closed doors for salary and benefit increases.

Before 2002, collective bargaining for state employees was limited to non-economic issues such as work conditions, while salary and benefit levels were determined through the normal budget process in the legislature.

Negotiating with the Governor in secret

Since the collective bargaining law went into full effect in 2004, union executives no longer have their priorities weighed equally with every other special interest during the legislative budget debate. Instead, they now negotiate directly with the Governor in secret, while lawmakers only have the opportunity to say "yes" or "no" to the entire contract agreed to with the Governor.

Not only are there serious transparency concerns with this arrangement, but there are also potential constitutional flaws by unduly restricting the legislature's constitutional authority to write the state budget.

When announcing the first secretly negotiated state employee contracts in 2004, Governor Gary Locke said:

"This year's contract negotiations mark the first time in state history that unions have been able to bargain with the state for wages and benefits. The new personnel reform law passed by the Legislature in 2002 expanded the state's collective bargaining activities to include wages and benefits. In the past, the Legislature unilaterally set those terms."[2]

Missing in this statement, however, is that this was also the first time in state history these spending decisions were not made in public. Governor Locke failed to note he had negotiated the contracts in secret, often with the same union executives who were his most important political supporters.

Secret talks on public spending violate the constitution

The decision made in 2002 that limited the authority of

2 "State, Unions Reach Tentative Agreement," press release, Office of Governor Gary Locke, September 13, 2004 at http://www.digitalarchives.wa.gov/ governorlocke/press/press-view.asp?pressReleas e=1689&newsType=1.

lawmakers to set priorities within the budget on state employee compensation should be reversed. This is especially important considering the compelling arguments made in the <u>University of Washington Law Review</u>, noting the 2002 law is an unconstitutional infringement on the legislature's authority to make budget decisions.[3]

Ultimately, state employee union contracts negotiated solely with the Governor should be limited to non-economic issues, like working conditions. Anything requiring an appropriation (especially new spending that relies on a tax increase) should be part of the normal open and public budget process in the legislature. This safeguard is especially important when public-sector unions are also political allies of the sitting Governor.

5. Policy Recommendation: End secret negotiations for public employee pay and benefits

Since 2004, as noted, the Governor has been granted the authority to negotiate secretly with union executives to determine how much taxpayers will pay for compensation to government employees. The secret talks involve government employee compensation totaling hundreds of millions in public spending per biennium.

Before 2004, those spending decisions were made in public as part of the normal legislative budget process, with the opportunity for comment at public hearings, before state officials made employee compensation promises.

---

3 "Stealing the Public Purse: Why Washington's Collective Bargaining Law for State Employees Violates the State Constitution," by Christopher D. Abbott, Washington Law Review, 2006-02, Volume 81, 2006, at https://digital.law. washington.edu/dspace-law/handle/1773.1/263.

Keeping lawmakers in the dark

Not only are public union contract negotiations conducted in secret, but none of the records are subject to public disclosure until after the contract is signed into law (when the budget is approved by the Governor). Lawmakers responsible for approving these contracts and the taxpayers who are asked to pay for them should not be kept in the dark until the deal is done and it is too late to make changes.

Some level of collective bargaining transparency is currently standard policy in nearly half of the states across the country. Some states open the entire negotiation process to the public, while others include an exemption when government officials are strategizing among themselves. Once public officials meet with union negotiators, however, the public is allowed to monitor the process.

This is exactly what occurs in Florida. As that state's Attorney General explains:

"The Legislature has, therefore, divided Sunshine Law policy on collective bargaining for public employees into two parts: when the public employer is meeting with its own side, it is exempt from the Sunshine Law; when the public employer is meeting with the other side, it is required to comply with the Sunshine Law."[4]

In Washington, these closed-door negotiations should be subject to the state's Open Public Meetings Act (OPMA) or at a minimum, utilize a process like the one used by the City of Costa

---

4 "Overview of the Sunshine and Public Records Law," Section D - What types of discussions are covered by the Sunshine Law?, Reporter's Handbook, the Florida Bar, accessed May 24, 2016, at https://www.floridabar.org/DIVCOM/PI/ RHandbook01.nsf/f5b2cbf2a827c0198525624b00057d30/07c774c1b21fa05585 2568a40074b173!OpenDocument#D.WHATTYPESOFDISCUSSIONSARE.

Mesa in California to keep the public informed. That process is called COIN (Civic Openness in Negotiations).

Under this system, all of the proposals and documents that are to be discussed in secret negotiations are made publicly available before and after meetings between the negotiating parties, with fiscal analysis provided showing the costs.

Informing the public about promises and trade-offs

While not full-fledged open meetings, providing access to all of the documents before meetings would inform the public about the promises and trade-offs being proposed with their tax dollars before an agreement is reached. This would also help make it clear whether one side or the other is being unreasonable, and would quickly reveal whether anyone, whether union executive or state official, is acting in bad faith.

There are several examples of collective bargaining transparency that already exist at the local level in Washington state. Examples include government union negotiations in Gig Harbor, Lincoln County, Kittitas County, Ferry County, Spokane County, the Pullman School District, and the Kennewick School District. [5]

Explaining why the Pullman School District embraces collective bargaining transparency, the district's finance manager Diane

---

5 "Kennewick School District opens the doors to collective bargaining," by Erin Shannon, blog post, Washington Policy Center, June 27, 2019, at https://www.washingtonpolicy.org/publications/detail/kennewick-school-district-opens-the-doors-to-collective-bargaining, and "Gig Harbor council asks for open labor negotiations," by Jake Gregg, *Tacoma News Tribune,* July 23, 2019, at https://www-1.thenewstribune.com/news/local/community/gateway/article233013217.html.

Hodge said, "We just think it's fair for all of the members to know what's being offered on both sides."[6]

Ending secrecy in government employee contract negotiations is popular. A statewide poll of 500 Washington voters conducted in 2015 found that 76% supported "requiring collective bargaining negotiations for government employers to be open to the public."[7]

Several newspaper editorials have also been written which call for government officials to open the doors to the public concerning government employment contracts. One such example is this editorial by *The Spokesman-Review*:[8]

"Bargainers say an open process would politicize the process and prevent frank discussions. These arguments are unpersuasive.

"It's already a political process, with the heavy influence of unions on the minds of governors, mayors and commissioners seeking re-election. The people left outside the door are paying for the decisions made by those inside. And we highly doubt honesty would go by the wayside if the public were watching. More likely, it would be cringe-inducing negotiating points that would go unspoken . . .

"The key question for government is: Do you trust the public? If the answer is no, don't expect it in return."

---

6 "Teacher-contract process needs transparent bargaining," editorial, The *Seattle Times*, August 29, 2018, at https://www.seattletimes.com/opinion/editorials/seattle-stalemate-shows-need-for-open-bargaining/.

7 Wickers Group statewide poll of 500 Washington voters, June 2015, copy available on request.

8 "Lincoln County leads way on government transparency," editorial, *The Spokesman Review*, September 18, 2016, at http://www.spokesman.com/stories/2016/sep/18/editorial-lincoln-county-leads-on-transparency/.

Conclusion

State and local employment contracts should not be negotiated in secret. The public provides money for these agreements. Taxpayers should be allowed to follow the process and hold government officials accountable for the spending decisions that officials make on their behalf.

6. Policy Recommendation: Restore the people's right of referendum by limiting the use of the emergency clause

To provide a check on the legislature, the state constitution grants the people the power to veto unwanted legislation through the use of a referendum. According to the secretary of state, "The referendum allows citizens, through the petition process, to refer acts of the legislature to the ballot before they become law."[9] This power applies to any bill adopted by the legislature except those that include an emergency clause.

An emergency clause states that a bill is exempt from repeal by referendum because the bill is, "necessary for the immediate preservation of the public peace, health or safety, support of the state government and its existing public institutions."[10] The use of the emergency clause allows bills to take effect immediately once signed by the governor.

Responding to public emergencies

The emergency clause allows the state government to respond

---

9 "Referendum Quick Facts," Elections and Voting, Washington Secretary of State, accessed May 24, 2016, at http://www.sos.wa.gov/elections/ReferendumQuickFacts.aspx.
10 "Constitution of the State of Washington," Article 2, Section 1, Legislative Information Center, revised January 12, 2011, at http://leg.wa.gov/lawsandagencyrules/documents/12-2010-wastateconstitution.pdf.

quickly to true public emergencies, like civil unrest or a natural disaster, yet lawmakers routinely abuse the exemption by attaching emergency clauses to routine bills. The result is that lawmakers often label unpopular political decisions as "emergencies" to shield themselves from public accountability.

The most effective way to end the legislature's abuse of the emergency clause is a constitutional amendment creating a supermajority vote requirement for its use. The legislature would then be prohibited from attaching an emergency clause unless the bill was approved by a 60 percent vote. This is enough to prevent political majorities from abusing the rule, while allowing the legislature to respond quickly to true public emergencies.

Budget bills, however, could be made exempt from the supermajority vote requirement, allowing them to pass with a simple majority and not be subject to a referendum.

Court labels a business deal a "public emergency"

Constitutional reforms are needed due to the state supreme court's granting of total deference to a legislative declaration of an emergency. The first opportunity the supreme court had to address the legislature's questionable use of an emergency clause was in 1995 with the passage of SB 6049, to provide public funding for the Mariners baseball stadium in Seattle.

In a 6-3 ruling upholding the denial of a people's referendum, the court said:

"Ultimately, the emergency that faced the Legislature was that the Seattle Mariners would be put up for sale on Oct. 30 (1995) unless, prior to that date, the Legislature enacted legislation that would assure the development of a new publicly owned baseball stadium for King County."[11]

For the first time, the court declared that a business deal involving a professional sports team fell under the definition of "public emergency." The supreme court had an opportunity to revisit this ruling in 2005 when a case raised the question of whether the legislature's suspension of a voter-approved limit on tax increases was a "public emergency" that required denying the people's right to a referendum.

Emergency clause as a blank check

Again, in a 6-3 ruling, the court upheld the legislature's declaration of an emergency.[12] The impact of the ruling was to give the legislature a blank check to use emergency clauses any time it wants. This has the effect of lawmakers routinely stripping the people of their right of referendum. The dissenting judges, however, wrote blistering objections to the majority's decision.

For example, Justice Richard Sanders warned that the ruling allows the legislature to avoid the people's right of referendum:

"Where the Legislature uses an emergency clause simply to avoid a referendum rather than respond in good faith to a true 'emergency'...and where the court essentially delegates its independent role as a constitutional guardian to the legislative branch of government in its power struggle against the popular branch of government; I find little left of the people's right of referendum."[13]

---

11 "Court Upholds Financing for New Ballpark," by David Postman, *The Seattle Times*, December 21, 1996, at http://community.seattletimes.nwsource.com/archive/?date=19961221&slug=2366157.
12 "Washington State Farm Bureau v. Reed," Washington State Supreme Court, July 14, 2005, at http://caselaw.findlaw.com/wa-supreme-court/1428354.html.
13 Ibid.

There is a better way to allow the legislature to respond to true emergencies while protecting the people's right of referendum. The following is from South Dakota's constitution (Article 3, Section 22):[14]

"Effective date of acts -- Emergency clause. No act shall take effect until ninety days after the adjournment of the session at which it passed, unless in case of emergency, (to be expressed in the preamble or body of the act) the Legislature shall by a vote of two-thirds of all the members elected of each house, otherwise direct."

Like South Dakota, Washington should also require a supermajority vote if lawmakers want to declare an emergency to prevent a referendum. Bills have been proposed in Olympia in previous years to do this but have not been adopted (see, for example, SJR 8206 from 2013).[15]

Political convenience and the people's rights

If a true public emergency occurs that warrants blocking the people's right to a referendum, a 60 percent vote requirement in the legislature should not be difficult to achieve. In the case of a real crisis, the public would most likely welcome the use of the emergency clause by the legislature, recognizing it is intended to be used at just such a critical time. Political convenience, however, should no longer serve as a reason to deny the people their right of referendum.

---

14 "South Dakota State Constitution," Secretary of State, accessed on August 20, 2019, at https://sdsos.gov/general-information/assets/2017SouthDakotaCons titution.pdf.

15 "SJR 8206, Amending the Constitution to require emergency clauses only be allowed by amendment to a bill and approved by sixty percent of each house of the legislature," Washington State Legislature, January 18, 2013, at https://app. leg.wa.gov/billsummary?BillNumber=8206&Year=2013&Initiative=false.

7. Policy Recommendation: Provide voters more information about the fiscal impact of ballot measures

Based on the recent passage of several budget-busting initiatives, there is a growing sense in the legislature that voters need more information about the fiscal impact of ballot measures before the election.

Just as when lawmakers consider a bill, voters should also take into consideration the financial effects of what they are being asked to approve. This is why the Office of Financial Management issues a fiscal note for each qualified ballot measure and includes that information in the voters' guide.16 Many voters, however, do not review this fiscal note carefully before casting their votes.

Providing greater transparency

One way to provide greater transparency on the financial effect of ballot measures is to put the estimated fiscal impact in the actual ballot language summary. The following is an example of how that language could look:

"OFM has determined this proposal would increase state spending by [dollar amount] without providing a revenue source. This means other state spending may be reduced or taxes increased to implement the proposal. Should this measure be enacted into law?"

This would complement the existing fiscal note the Office of Financial Management provides on ballot measures, while putting the financial implications of the measure in the ballot title, so it is directly before voters.

---

16 "Revised Code of Washington 29A.72.025 - Fiscal impact statements," effective date July 1, 2004, Washington State Legislature http://apps.leg.wa.gov/RCW/default.aspx?cite=29A.72.025.

After being informed about how much a ballot measure will cost, and voters still decide to push spending far beyond what existing revenue will sustain, lawmakers could still balance the budget with a two-thirds vote to change, repeal or temporarily suspend the voter-approved limit on tax increases.

8. Policy Recommendation: Adopt constitutional amendment prohibiting unfunded mandates on local governments

Washington voters have repeatedly adopted tax and spending restrictions to control state spending growth and force budget prioritization to avoid unnecessary tax increases.

Though these tax restrictions have since been thrown out by the state Supreme Court, the budget requirements passed by voters remain in law. This includes the prohibition on the legislature from imposing unfunded mandates on local governments. If unfunded mandates are against state law, why are local governments still being subjected to them?

Commenting on his growing frustration with unfunded mandates and the lack of understanding from the legislature, Lincoln County Commissioner Scott Hutsell said, "We are providing these services on behalf of the State. I think sometimes we get treated like foreign countries."[17]

Based on ballot measures adopted by voters in 1979 and 1993, however, unfunded mandates on local government should not be occurring. Here is the ballot summary for Initiative 62, adopted in 1979 to control state tax revenue growth:

---

17 "State law prohibits unfunded mandates, yet local governments continue to be burdened by them," by Jason Mercier, Washington Policy Center, April 10, 2018, at https://www.washingtonpolicy.org/publications/detail/state-law-prohibits-unfunded-mandates-yet-local-governments-continue-to-be-burdened-by-them.

"This limit would apply only to the state – not to local governments. The initiative, however, would prohibit the legislature from requiring local governments to offer new or expanded services unless the costs are paid by the state."[18]

Section 6 of Initiative 62 explicitly provided:

"(1) The legislature shall not impose responsibility for new programs or increased levels of service under existing programs on any taxing district unless the districts are reimbursed for the costs thereof by the state."

After Initiative 62 failed to control state tax and spending increases adequately, the voters adopted Initiative 601 in 1993. Along with imposing new tax and spending limits, the ballot summary for Initiative 601 noted:

"The Legislature would be prohibited from imposing responsibility for new programs or increased levels of service on any political subdivision of the state, unless the subdivision is fully reimbursed by specific appropriation by the state."[19]

The combination of Initiative 62 and Initiative 601 restrictions on unfunded mandates makes up the current state prohibition found in state law:

". . . the legislature shall not impose responsibility for new programs or increased levels of service under existing programs on any political subdivision of the state unless the

---

18 "1979 Voters Pamphlet – General Election November 6," Washington Secretary of State, at https://www.sos.wa.gov/_assets/elections/voters'%20 pamphlet%201979.pdf.
19 "State of Washington Voters Pamphlet – General Election November 2, 1993," Washington Secretary of State, at https://www.sos.wa.gov/_assets/ elections/voters'%20pamphlet%201993.pdf.

subdivision is fully reimbursed by the state for the costs of the new programs or increases in service levels." [20]

The intent of voters was clear in adopting these two initiatives. State spending and taxes should be restricted, and local governments protected, so lawmakers do not simply shift the cost of programs and expect local officials to raise taxes to fund them. Unfortunately, that is exactly what is happening today.

Rather than comply with state law that prohibits unfunded mandates, the response from lawmakers appears to be to give local governments new taxing authority or weaken other tax protections like the voter-approved cap on property taxes.

Since the current voter-approved law prohibiting unfunded mandates is not working, legislators should consider how other states protect their local governments. In 1995, New Jersey voters adopted the "State Mandate, State Pay" constitutional amendment. Unlike Washington's oft-ignored statutory ban, the New Jersey constitutional amendment has an enforcement mechanism to ensure compliance:

> "The Legislature shall create by law a Council on Local Mandates. The Council shall resolve any dispute regarding whether a law or rule or regulation issued pursuant to a law constitutes an unfunded mandate."

According to the New Jersey Council on Local Mandates:

> "The Council, which began operations in 1996, is a bipartisan body that is independent of the Executive, Legislative and Judicial branches of State government . . . Council deliberations begin with the filing of a complaint by a county,

---

20 Revised Code of Washington 43.135.060, "Prohibition of new or extended programs without full reimbursement – Transfer of programs – Determination of costs."

municipality, or school board, or by a county executive or mayor who has been directly elected by voters."[21]

Lawmakers easily ignore the Washington state law barring imposition of unfunded local mandates. This is the exact situation voters tried to prevent when they passed Initiative 62 and Initiative 601. The goal was to force fiscal discipline on the state while preventing costs and pressure for tax increases to be shifted to local governments.

Especially in a time of record state revenues and spending, the answer to unfunded mandates is not to tell local officials to raise taxes, but instead for lawmakers to direct state spending within existing revenue to comply with the law. The ongoing failure of lawmakers to do so, however, shows that additional protections against unfunded mandates are needed for local officials and taxpayers.

---

21 "State of New Jersey Council on Local Mandates," accessed on August 20, 2019, at https://www.state.nj.us/localmandates/amendment/.

Spending

Additional resources

"Should it be easy to declare a referendum-killing 'emergency'?" by Jason Mercier, Washington Policy Center, March 7, 2019

"Revenue forecast shows it's time for a sales tax cut, by Jason Mercier, Legislative Memo, Washington Policy Center, January 2019

"Transparency in public employee collective bargaining: How Washington compares to other states," by Erin Shannon, Policy Brief, Washington Policy Center, December 2018

"Budget reforms are needed to end the threat of state government shut-downs," by Jason Mercier, Policy Notes, Washington Policy Center, September 2015

"Changing the budget status quo," by Paul Guppy and Jason Mercier, Policy Notes, Washington Policy Center, December 2008

CHAPTER TWO
REFORMING TAXATION

1. Policy Recommendation: Support Washington families by enacting tax relief

The proper purpose of taxation is to raise money to fund the core functions of government in a neutral way. A "fair field and no favors" is a good motto for a strong tax system, one without political favors or carve-outs for privileged interest groups. A principled tax system promotes social justice because it treats all citizens equally, regardless of social standing, insider dealing or political influence.

The following tax principles provide guidance for a fair and effective tax system; one that raises needed revenue for basic government services, while minimizing the financial burden lawmakers impose on their fellow citizens:

- Simplicity
- Accountability
- Economic Neutrality
- Equity
- Complementary
- Competitiveness
- Reliability
- Transparency

Washington's current tax structure provides reliable revenue growth. Though there is no recession-proof tax structure, Washington consistently ranks as having relatively stable tax collections compared to other states. The reason is that Washington's three major tax sources (sales, gross receipts, and property) are among the least volatile elements of the economy. Data shows, however, that a graduated income tax is among the most volatile of revenue sources.

Standard & Poor's have also noted the relative stability of Washington's tax collections. From the rating firm's August 2019 bond rating for the state:

- "Good recent economic growth relative to that of the nation and a sales tax-based revenue structure that has demonstrated less sensitivity to economic cycles than income tax-reliant states;"

- "Washington's revenues have historically exhibited less cyclicality than others (due in part to lack of personal income tax);"

- "The state's reliance on retail sales and business and occupation taxes typically affords Washington more revenue stability than other states that rely on personal income tax revenues;"

- "In addition, we have observed that capital gains-related tax revenues are among the most cyclical and difficult to forecast revenues in numerous other states."[1]

Though fairly reliable, Washington tax structure is often criticized for having an undue effect on families, compared to businesses. This concern is the result of how lawmakers have layered on new taxation over the years while providing little tax

---

1 "State of Washington, Appropriations, General Obligation," Standard & Poor's Global Ratings, by analysts Jillian Legnos and Oscar Padilla, August 28, 2019, at https://www.tre.wa.gov/wp-content/uploads/2020ABT-R-2020AB-SP-2019.08.28-Report.pdf.

relief. The people of Washington now pay over 50 different kinds of taxes at the state and local level.[2]

Further, Washington has some of the highest excise taxes in the nation. The state's sales tax rate has not been reduced since 1982. One tax, in particular, the Motor Vehicle Excise Tax (MVET), is in need of reform because officials do not tax the true value of cars and trucks, instead using inflated values that result in a higher tax.

MVET viewed as unfair

The MVET is imposed by the Sound Transit agency in King, Pierce and Snohomish counties, where the majority of Washington residents live. Many families pay the MVET many times in one year because officials apply it to a wide range of vehicles, including cars, trucks, motorcycles, motor homes and trailers. Some families pay the tax on as many as five or six different vehicles and trailers every year, resulting in hundreds of dollars in cost per family.

In addition to the high tax burden imposed on families, the MVET is considered unfair because of the artificial method officials use to set a vehicle's value. Officials use an inflated value schedule, instead of true market value, to decide the tax burden they impose on vehicle owners. This results in the overvaluing of most vehicles, which enables Sound Transit officials to take more tax revenue from the public unfairly.

Further, some cities impose a car tab tax through a local Transportation Benefit Districts (TBDs), but these are flat fees that everyone pays equally regardless of the type of vehicle.

---

2 "The Tax Reference Manual, Information on State and Local Taxes in Washington State," by Kathy Oline, Assistant Director, compiled by Don Taylor, Research Division, Washington State Department of Revenue, January 2010, at http://dor.wa.gov/docs/reports/2010/Tax_Reference_2010/TRM%202010%20 -%20Entire%20Document.pdf.

Legitimate car tab taxes, whether an MVET or through a TBD, should only fund roads used by the general public. Taxes for transit, which is already richly funded, should be broad-based and approved separately by voters.

State sales tax rate has not been reduced since 1982

In addition to heavy vehicle taxes, state and local officials impose a high sales tax on Washington residents. The total state and local rate on consumer purchases, except food and medicine, often exceeds ten percent, one of the highest rates in the country.

In King County, officials impose the highest sales tax rate in the state, making it harder to find work and earn a living in otherwise prosperous urban communities. By imposing a high sales tax rate, public officials force Washingtonians to devote an ever-larger share of household income to funding government agencies and subsidizing public programs.

When it was first imposed in 1935, the state sales tax rate was just two percent, a modest rate that most families could afford. The state tax is currently 6.5 percent, with local sales taxes added on top, and citizens have not seen a rate reduction since 1982, as illustrated to the right.

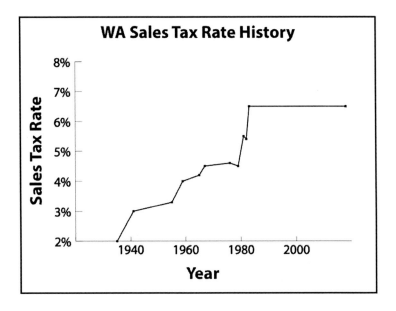

Washington state sales tax rate started at just 2%. Since then, lawmakers have more than tripled the tax burden to 6.5 percent.

Recently the federal courts have expanded the sales tax by ruling, in the *Wayfair* case, that state lawmakers can tax out-of-state businesses.[3] The larger tax base, the growing state economy and continued large increases in state revenue growth mean that lawmakers are in a good position to provide sales tax relief for Washington families.

Providing property tax relief

As lawmakers and local officials increase total property collections, they increase the amount each property owner must pay. In addition, local officials often ask voters for special levies, saying tax increases are needed to pay for essential public services, even when regular property tax revenue is already increasing. When levies are framed as preventing cuts in schools, parks and

---

3 *South Dakota v. Wayfair, Inc.*, United States Supreme Court, decided June 21, 2018, at https://www.supremecourt.gov/opinions/17pdf/17-494_j4el.pdf.

medical services, people feel pressured to vote "yes," despite the higher cost.

The result is a rising financial burden that falls hardest on people living on fixed incomes, the elderly, the disabled and the unemployed. Public officials should manage the normal increases in regular tax collections responsibly, or use it to provide tax relief, rather than seeking more money by increasing the financial burden they place on the most vulnerable people in the community.

2. Policy Recommendation: Adopt a constitutional amendment requiring a supermajority vote to raise taxes

In February 2013, the state supreme court overturned the voter-approved requirement that proposed tax increases must receive a supermajority vote of the legislature, or voter approval, to be enacted. When the supreme court strikes down a law passed by the people, the legislature often seeks to implement what the people want.

Recent examples include Initiative 695, to reduce car tab costs, and Initiative 747, to limit yearly property tax increases. In both cases, after the courts ruled against popular ballot initiatives, lawmakers of both parties joined together to pass bills that carried out the will of the voters.

Ballot measures to limit tax increases consistently receive strong voter support. Approval of Initiative 1366 in 2015 represented the sixth time in 26 years that voters have approved the policy of requiring a supermajority vote in the legislature to pass tax increases. Voters passed similar measures in 1993, 1998, 2007, 2010 and 2012. In addition, in 1979 voters approved a revenue limit based on the growth in state personal income (Initiative 62), which required a supermajority vote of lawmakers to exceed the limit.[4]

Supermajority vote requirements are common

Requiring a supermajority vote in the legislature to increase taxes is not unique to Washington. Seventeen states have some form of supermajority vote requirement for tax increases. Supermajority requirements are common in provisions of Washington's constitution.

There are currently more than 20 supermajority vote requirements in the state's constitution. Several of these provisions have been part of the Washington constitution since statehood. The most recent one was added by lawmakers, and confirmed by voters, in 2007.

A supermajority vote requirement is not undemocratic

Since supermajority vote restrictions are a common way for the people to place limits on government power, lawmakers should send voters a proposed constitutional amendment to require a supermajority vote in the legislature to raise taxes. Such a proposal would not be undemocratic. Instead, it would be consistent with existing constitutional precedents for requiring higher vote thresholds for certain government actions.

A statewide poll in 2016 found that 65 percent of voters want lawmakers to send them a constitutional amendment requiring a

---

4 Initiative 62, "Limitation on State Tax Revenues," List of All Initiatives to the People and List of All Referendum Measures, at Initiative and Referendum History and Statistics, Washington Secretary of State, at https://www.sos. wa.gov/elections/initiatives/statistics.aspx, accessed September 4, 2019.

supermajority vote to raise taxes.[5] Voters and lawmakers clearly want reasonable limits on raising taxes. Passage of a constitutional amendment would set this popular commonsense policy in place and decide the matter once and for all, without further interference by the courts.

3. Policy Recommendation: Do not impose a state income tax, including an income tax on capital gains

Washington is one of only seven states that do not tax personal incomes (two other states do not tax general income but have narrow taxes on interest). Doing so would fundamentally alter Washington state's tax structure, changing it from one that mainly taxes consumption to one that also taxes people's work and productivity.

Each of the 50 states levies a different combination of taxes on the people who live, work or travel within its borders. These different types and levels of taxation have a profound effect on the actions of residents and business owners, and taxation can significantly impede opportunities and economic growth personally. More than any other type of tax, an income tax can stifle a state's economic growth, de-stabilize public finances and limit people's take-home pay.

A graduated income tax is unconstitutional in Washington

Since 1933, the Washington state supreme court has issued several opinions on Article 7, Sections 1 and 2 of the state constitution to require taxation of property, which includes income, to be uniform and limited to a rate of one percent. For example,

___

5 "New Poll: Lawmakers should act on supermajority for taxes amendment," by Lisa Shin, press release, Washington Policy Center, January 5, 2016, at http://www.washingtonpolicy.org/publications/detail/new-poll-lawmakers-should-act-on-supermajority-for-taxes-amendment.

the state supreme court ruled in 1951, "It is no longer subject to question in this court that income is property."

While there is no ban on a flat income tax of one percent, nearly 90 years of legal precedents show that a graduated or targeted income tax that treats people with different income levels differently is considered unfair and unconstitutional in Washington.

Despite these repeated rulings from the state supreme court, income tax proponents say these rulings are "antiquated." Faced with this argument in 1960, the state supreme court ruled:

"The argument is again pressed upon us that these cases were wrongly decided. The court is unwilling, however, to recede from the position announced in its repeated decisions. Among other things, the attorney general urges that the result should now be different because the state is confronted with a financial crisis. If so, the constitution may be amended by vote of the people."[6]

With the voters unwilling to amend the constitution to allow an income tax, income tax tax-increase advocates are again trying to get the judges to reverse their past rulings.

A state income tax is unpopular

Lawmakers should send voters a crystal clear state constitutional amendment banning income taxes in Washington. Based on past elections, the people clearly oppose a state income tax in Washington, and a proposed ban would probably pass. Washington voters have overwhelmingly rejected income tax proposals ten times, including six proposed constitutional amendments.

---

6 "Timeless advice from WA Supreme Court on income taxes," by Jason Mercier, Washington Policy Center, September 6, 2017, at https://www. washingtonpolicy.org/publications/detail/timeless-advice-from-wa-supreme-court-on-income-taxes.

Here is the record of popular opposition to measures proposing a state income tax:

- 1934 – House Joint Resolution 11........ defeated 43% to 57%
- 1936 – Senate Joint Resolution 7 .... defeated 22% to 78%
- 1938 – Senate Joint Resolution 5 .... defeated 33% to 67%
- 1942 – Constitutional Amendment ..... defeated 34% to 66%
- 1944 – Initiative 158 .... defeated 30% to 70%
- 1970 – House Joint Resolution 42 .... defeated 32% to 68%
- 1973 – House Joint Resolution 37 .... defeated 23% to 77%
- 1975 – Initiative 314 .... defeated 33% to 67%
- 1982 – Initiative 435 .... defeated 34% to 66%
- 2010 – Initiative 1098 .... defeated 36% to 64%

In Tennessee, lawmakers wanted to assure citizens that imposing a state income tax was not just one legislative session away. They asked voters to approve a constitutional amendment banning income taxes. As the sponsor of the Tennessee income tax ban explained:

> "This is going to help us bring in jobs to Tennessee. We can say not only do we not have an income tax, but we'll never have an income tax."[7]

In 2014, Tennessee voters passed the proposal with 66 percent of the vote, and the state's constitutional ban on a state income tax went into effect.

As in Tennessee, lawmakers in Washington should let the people vote on a constitutional amendment that makes our state's ban on an income tax clear while protecting the ban from being

---

7 "Senate OKs measure to ban Tenn. income tax," by Lucas Johnson II, *Business Week,* March 9, 2011.

overturned by a surprise court ruling in which judges ignore past legal precedents.

Capital gains taxes are income taxes

Some politicians have called for imposing a state capital gains income tax on the people of Washington state. They claim, however, this type of tax is an "excise tax" and not an income tax, in hopes of getting around the state constitution's prohibition on graduated income taxes.

Every state revenue department in the country, however, classifies a capital gains tax as an income tax. Those that tax capital gains do so through their income tax codes. No state taxes capital gains as an "excise tax." All states without a capital gains tax have one factor in common – no personal income tax.

In response to a congressional inquiry, here is the Internal Revenue Service (IRS) description of a capital gains tax:

> "You ask whether tax on capital gains is considered an excise tax or an income tax? It is an income tax. More specifically, capital gains are treated as income under the tax code and taxed as such."[8]

Washington's nonpartisan legislative staff agrees, stating in a bill report for one capital gains tax proposal:

> "In addition to the federal tax, capital gains are often subject to state income taxes. Most states do not have separate capital

---

8 Letter from U.S. Department of the Treasury, Internal Revenue Service to U.S. Representative Dan Newhouse, September 25, 2018, quoted in "IRS: Capital gains tax 'is an income tax'," by Jason Mercier, Washington Policy Center, September 25, 2018.

gains tax rates. Instead, most states tax capital gains as ordinary income subject to the state's income tax rates."[9]

Capital gains income taxes are unstable

Besides being unconstitutional, a capital gains income tax is bad budget policy. The volatile history of capital gains income taxes in other states shows this form of taxation does not provide fiscally sound revenue for government services.

As warned by former California Governor Jerry Brown, income taxes on capital gains are extremely volatile. Heeding Governor Brown's recommendation, California voters in 2014 approved a constitutional amendment to restrict the use of capital gains for state spending.

Explaining the impact of the constitutional amendment, the California Legislative Analyst's Office (LAO) said: "This constitutional amendment separates state spending from the rollercoaster of revenue volatility."

In addition, California's LAO report states:

"Probably the single most direct way to limit the state's exposure to the kind of extreme revenue volatility experienced in the past decade would be to reduce its dependence on the source of income that produced the greatest portion of this revenue volatility – namely, capital gains and perhaps stock options."[10]

---

9 "SB 5129, increasing revenues for the support of state government," Senate bill Report, Washington State Legislature, January 14, 2019, at http://lawfilesext. leg.wa.gov/biennium/2019-20/Pdf/Bill%20Reports/Senate/5129%20SBA%20 WM%2019.pdf.
10 "Revenue Volatility in California," by Elizabeth G. Hill, Legislative Analyst, California Legislative Analyst's Office, January 2005, at http://www.lao. ca.gov/2005/rev_vol/rev_volatility_012005.pdf.

Researchers at Standard and Poor's found that "State tax revenue trends have also become more volatile as progressive tax states have come to rely more heavily on capital gains from top earners."[11]

Similarly, analysts at the Washington State Department of Revenue found that:

> "Capital gains are extremely volatile from year to year. Revenue from this proposal will depend entirely on fluctuations in the financial markets and can be expected to vary greatly from the amounts presented here."[12]

Officials point to the benefit of no state capital gains income tax

Government officials in Washington state recognize the public benefit of not taxing capital gains. The state Department of Commerce noted that in Washington:

> "We offer businesses some competitive advantages found in few other states. These include no taxes on capital gains or personal or corporate income. We also offer industry-specific tax breaks to spur innovation and growth whenever possible."[13]

Department of Commerce officials warned that if an income tax is imposed it would mean "one less tool that we have in our economic development toolbox."

---

11 "Income Inequality Weighs On State Tax Revenues," S&P Capital IQ, Global Credit Portal, Standard and Poor's, September 15, 2014.
12 "Fiscal Note for HB 2563: Establishing a state tax on capital gains," Washington State Legislature, February 2, 2012.
13 "Choose Washington – Pro-Business," Washington State Department of Commerce, February 8, 2015 at https://web.archive.org/web/20121213195601/ http://choosewashingtonstate.com/why-washington/our-strengths/pro-business/.

For these reasons, lawmakers should maintain Washington's competitive advantage and not adopt a highly volatile, and likely unconstitutional, capital gains income tax.

4. Policy Recommendation: Affirm the state ban on local income taxes

In 1984 the state legislature adopted RCW 36.65.030, "Tax on net income prohibited." Acknowledging this clear restriction on a local income tax, the City Attorney of Seattle reported in a 2014 legal analysis that cities do not have the authority to impose a local income tax.[14]

Despite this clear prohibition, in 2017, the Seattle City Council enacted one anyway in hopes of persuading the courts to ignore their prior rulings and allow a local income tax.[15] As expected, a King County Superior Court judge immediately invalidated Seattle's income tax saying it was clearly illegal under state law.[16] The Court of Appeals, however, issued a surprising decision on July 15, 2019 in this case.

The Court of Appeals did rule unanimously that Seattle's graduated income tax was unconstitutional, based on the numerous state supreme court decisions. Surprisingly, however, the court also invalidated the prohibition on local governments imposing a

---

14 "City of Seattle Attorney in 2014: 'The legislature has not granted cities the authority to impose an income tax,'" by Jason Mercier, Washington Policy Center, April 18, 2019, at https://www.washingtonpolicy.org/publications/detail/city-of-seattle-attorney-in-2014-the-legislature-has-not-granted-cities-the-authority-to-impose-an-income-tax.

15 "Timeless advice from WA Supreme Court on income taxes," by Jason Mercier, blogpost, Washington Policy Center, September 6, 2017, at https://www.washingtonpolicy.org/publications/detail/timeless-advice-from-wa-supreme-court-on-income-taxes.

16 "Judge rules Seattle income tax illegal," by Jason Mercier, blogpost, Washington Policy Center, November 22, 2017, at https://www.washingtonpolicy.org/publications/detail/judge-rules-seattle-income-tax-illegal.

---

flat income tax. This ruling means officials in cities may be able to impose a flat local income tax pending review by the state supreme court.

Many lawmakers say they oppose an income tax, but they took no action on HB 1588 during the 2019 Legislative session. HB 1588 provides:

> "The Legislature restates its refusal to delegate to a city, county, or city-county, as a whole or as a governing body, the power to impose a tax on the personal income of individuals or households . . . This prohibition, and the definition of income specifically, are to be construed broadly by any reviewing court to affect the policy of this state that there exist absolute clarity and certainty in state law that there is no local government authority to levy any form of income tax on individuals or households."[17]

Conclusion

Banning local income taxes would serve the public interest by helping to maintain the state's competitive advantage of having no income taxes. Lawmakers should re-affirm the state ban on local income taxes to discourage local officials from trying to imitate Seattle's legal games.

5. Policy Recommendation: Replace the Business and Occupation tax with a Single Business Tax

Washington's Department of Revenue defines the Business and Occupation (B&O) tax as a tax on "gross receipts of all business operating in Washington, for the privilege of engaging in business." Gross receipts refers to total yearly business income,

---

17 "HB 1588: Clarifying the prohibition of the imposition of a local income tax," Washington State Legislature, January 24, 2019, at https://app.leg.wa.gov/billsummary? BillNumber=1588&Initiative=false&Year=2019.

the total value of sales, or the total value of products, whichever is applicable. The B&O tax is the second-largest source of revenue for the state, after the sales tax.

As a levy on gross receipts, the B&O tax does not allow business owners to deduct the cost of doing business, such as the payments they make for materials, rent, equipment or wages, when they calculate how much they must pay.

It is important to remember the B&O tax was originally adopted as a "temporary" emergency tax in response to the Great Depression. In 1933 the state supreme court upheld the tax, saying:

"This law is, perhaps, not perfect. No tax law yet devised has been entirely fair and just to all in its practical workings. This is an emergency measure, limited by its terms to a two-year period. If it works injustice to some, it will be but temporary, and such temporary injustice, if any, must be borne for the common good."[18]

A system riddled with preferences

The B&O tax creates severe distortions and puts Washington employers, especially small and start-up businesses, at a competitive disadvantage. To try to mitigate this unfairness, the legislature has passed numerous special deductions, credits and exemptions as a benefit to some industries. At the same time, lawmakers have raised B&O tax rates in order to increase revenue while giving some industries favored treatment. The result is a complex system of high tax rates riddled with hundreds of preferences and special exemptions.

---

18 *State ex rel. Stiner v. Yelle*, Washington State Supreme Court, September 8, 1933, at http://courts.mrsc.org/washreports/174WashReport/174WashRepo rt0402.htm.

There is a better way - a simple, fair Single Business Tax. While based on total receipts like the B&O tax, a Single Business Tax would eliminate the current system's unfair and confusing tangle of tax rates and preferences and replace it with a simplified system that treats all business owners equally and uses one fair, flat rate.

How it would work

Each year business owners would choose one of three ways to calculate how much tax they owe, and they would be allowed to use the method that results in the lowest tax burden. Business owners would calculate their tax based on:

1. Total gross receipts minus labor costs, or;

2. Total gross receipts minus all production costs except labor, or;

3. 60 percent of total gross receipts.

To find the dollar amount of tax owed, the business owner would then multiply the taxable receipts by the Single Business Tax rate. Cities could levy their own business taxes, but the same uniformity standard would apply – any local business tax would have to be based on a single rate applied equally to all business owners, with no loopholes, special exemptions or political favoritism.

The business owner would send the final amount owed for each taxing jurisdiction to the state in one payment. State officials would then place the revenue from the state business tax in the treasury and distribute the local business tax revenue to different local governments.

A simpler, fairer tax

This proposal would eliminate today's confusing list of over 40 tax rates that state officials now impose on business activities every year. It would repeal the layers of special-interest tax credits and exemptions that have built up over the decades and would provide relief to small businesses with low profitability. The Single Business Tax could be phased in over several years to allow time for citizens and policymakers to adjust to the new system.

Conclusion

Enacting a Single Business Tax would bring simplicity, equity and fairness to Washington's tax code. It would end thousands of hours of compliance time for business owners and ordinary citizens, and encourage job creation and economic growth, while providing the Governor and lawmakers with reliable revenue to fund the core services of government.

6. Policy Recommendation: Create a tax transparency website like the fiscal.wa.gov site

There are approximately 1,800 taxing districts in the state whose officials impose various taxes on Washingtonians.[19] There is no single resource, however, to help individuals and businesses learn which taxing districts and rates they are subject to, and how much officials in each taxing district add to their total tax burden. A typical home, for example, can be located in as many as ten different taxing districts.

To help improve the transparency of state and local taxation, state leaders should create an online searchable database of all tax districts and tax rates in the state. The database could be modeled after the state's high-quality budget transparency website: fiscal. wa.gov.

If enacted by state officials, this recommendation would set up

19 "Bipartisan state tax transparency website bill proposed," by Jason Mercier, Washington Policy Center, January 28, 2019, at https://www.washingtonpolicy. org/publications/detail/bipartisan-state-tax-transparency-website-bill-proposed.

an online database where citizens could find their state and local tax rates (such as property and sales taxes) by entering a zip code, street address, or by clicking on a map showing individual taxing district boundaries.

Enhancing trust in government

A non-binding online calculator would allow individuals and business owners to estimate their total tax burden and know which officials are responsible for imposing each tax. To facilitate a searchable database, taxing districts would report their tax rates to the state annually and report any changes in their tax rates within 30 days of imposing rate changes.

SB 6032 Sec 135 (4) of the 2018 Supplemental Budget would have created a tax transparency website (SB 6590). Within days of the bill's passage, however, the tax transparency section was vetoed by Governor Inslee.

Increasing the ease of public access to state and local tax rates would enhance trust in government and increase the public's understanding of the cost of government services. Improved transparency would also promote healthy tax competition among geographic areas. Citizens could compare different tax burdens imposed by local officials, based on where they decide to live or locate their businesses.

Conclusion

Lawmakers should again pass this bipartisan proposal to create an online searchable website of all tax districts and tax rates in the state and urge the Governor to sign this popular commonsense measure.

Additional resources

"How to reform Washington's tax structure," by Jason Mercier, Policy Brief, Washington Policy Center, March 2019

"Call capital-gains tax for what it really is – an income tax," by Jason Mercier, *The Seattle Times*, March 29, 2019

"Bipartisan state tax transparency website bill proposed," by Jason Mercier, Washington Policy Center, January 28, 2019

"SJR 8208 and SJR 8209, to amend the state constitution to require a two-thirds vote in the legislature to raise taxes," by Jason Mercier, Legislative Memo, Washington Policy Center, January 2016

"Proposed capital gains tax is likely an unconstitutional income tax and would be an unreliable revenue source," by Jason Mercier, Legislative Memo, Washington Policy Center, March 2015

"History of Washington state tax ballot measures since 1932," by Jason Mercier, Legislative Memo, Washington Policy Center, January 2012

CHAPTER THREE
PROTECTING THE ENVIRONMENT

1. Policy Recommendation: Empower individuals with smartphone environmental solutions

In a world where smartphones and the internet connect everyone, environmental activism is stuck in the 1970s, and the immediate impulse is to use the same approach today that we chose in the 1970s, when we created the Environmental Protection Agency and creating the Clean Air Act and the Clean Water Act.

A half-century later, however, there are many new technology options, and the nature of environmental problems are now very different. Former Environmental Protection Agency Administrator William Ruckelshaus notes, "We have made little or no progress on non-point-source pollution. In fact, the EPA's latest estimate is that the percentage impact on receiving waters is just the reverse of that in 1970: 15% of the problem is point sources of pollution, and 85% of the impact is non-point sources."

Smartphones and personal technology offer the ability to address these distributed environmental problems better than centralized government agencies. Rather than immediately turning to the government for environmental solutions, smartphone environmentalism offers a better way to address many of our most difficult environmental problems.

Giving power to people with incentives to conserve

Market prices send strong signals about the value of resources, providing incentives to conserve while saving money. For example, Nest thermostats allow homeowners to save money while reducing energy demand during high-cost hours when utilities pay the most for electricity. Nest users in some areas can choose to participate in programs that automatically adjust your thermostat to save energy during critical parts of the day.

Southern California Edison (SCE) tested the effectiveness of Nest thermostats at reducing peak demand and found Nest thermostats, combined with price incentives, "significantly increased the magnitude of peak load reductions relative to the first summer [of the test period]." Simply giving people information and a tool to respond to the incentives they already have worked to shift demand and reduce energy costs.

Electricity use is not the only area in which smartphone technology can save resources. A new technology called Buoy connects to a house's water line and provides users more information about how they use water and gives them increased control.

By tracking where the water goes, Buoy provides information that helps users find ways to conserve. Buoy's creators found homeowners typically waste about 9.5 percent of the water their homes receive. Fixing those household leaks would save up to 13,000 gallons of water a year, saving hundreds of dollars.

Collaborating to help the environment

Smartphones and the internet also connect people, allowing them to combine information and tackle environmental problems. For example, an app called eBird helped create habitat for migratory birds simply by collecting data from a wide network of birdwatchers.

Using the existing data from eBird checklists, The Nature Conservancy (TNC) was able to identify land in California most used by the birds as they migrated.

Once they had the information, TNC went to the California Rice Commission and farmers, offering to pay them to create "pop-up habitats" for short periods. TNC offered to pay farmers to flood their fields with a few inches of water and leave them idle during a time when they might otherwise be preparing for the next growing season. Farmers agreed, named their price, and TNC rented the land to create migratory habitat.

Smartphones reduce what Nobel Prizewinning economic Ronald Coase called "transaction costs," the cost of sharing information and collaborating.

For distributed environmental problems, like those identified by Ruckelshaus, smartphone information aggregation is a critical part of identifying problems and opportunities in ways that have not been available before.

Smartphone environmental opportunities

Smartphones can also improve the efficiency of government. One example is King County's new noxious weed app, which allows users to photograph, identify, and report noxious weeds.[1] Photos can be assessed by King County staff without a site visit. Previously, users had to submit a written report with vague descriptions of the location and the plant. The new app saves time and money by improving the quality of information shared by users.

Conclusion

Smartphone technology can empower people who have incentives to save resources. By allowing users to track electricity and water use, they can conserve energy and avoid waste. Unlike

---

1 "Noxious weeds? Now there's an app for that in King County," by Paige Cornwall, *The Seattle Times,* June 18, 2019, at https://www.seattletimes.com/seattle-news/noxious-weeds-now-theres-an-app-for-that-in-king-county/.

many politicians, individuals will admit when they have made a mistake and find ways to change their behavior to save money.

Rather than simply turning to expanded government programs that are unable to solve many of today's environmental problems, policymakers, innovators, and the public should use the power we now have in the palm of our hand.

2. Policy Recommendation: Destroying the Snake River dams would be bad for the economy and the environment

In 1999, environmental activists paid for a full-page ad in *The New York Times* claiming that unless the four Lower Snake River Dams were removed, "wild Snake River spring chinook salmon, once the largest run of its kind in the world, will be extinct by 2017." Instead, adult Chinook returns average more than five times as many fish per year than in the decade before the ad ran.

Despite increased fish populations, some in the environmental community are still calling for destroying the Snake River dams. Focus on the dams is a dangerous distraction from the real work that needs to be done to help salmon populations across the Northwest.

Destroying dams won't save salmon or orca

National Oceanic and Atmospheric Administration (NOAA) Fisheries notes that the dams are "very close to achieving, or have already achieved, the juvenile dam passage survival objective of 96 percent for yearling Chinook salmon and steelhead migrants."[2] At best, destroying the dams would increase the current survival rate by a very small amount.

NOAA Fisheries' recovery plan notes that some risks to salmon will decrease without the dams, but others may increase. Dr. Peter Kareiva, who analyzed the impact of the Snake River dams for NOAA Fisheries in the early 2000s, argues, "it is not certain that dams now cause higher mortality than would arise in a free-flowing river." He concludes that "it has become clear that salmon conservation is being used as a 'means to an end' (dam removal) as opposed to an 'end' of its own accord."[3]

With the declining population of Southern Resident Killer Whales in Puget Sound, some argue that destroying the dams would help them recover. In 2018, NOAA Fisheries and the Washington State Department of Fish and Wildlife ranked the watersheds based on their importance to orca recovery. They determined that the Snake River ranked 9th in importance behind the Puget Sound, the Frasier River, Lower Columbia and other regions.[4].

2 "ESA Snake River Spring/Summer Chinook Salmon and Snake River Basin Steelhead Recovery Plan," NOA Fisheries, November 2017, at https://www.westcoast.fisheries.noaa.gov/publications/recovery_planning/salmon_steelhead/domains/interior_columbia/snake/Final%20Snake%20Recovery%20Plan%20Docs/final_snake_river_spring-summer_chinook_salmon_and_snake_river_basin_steelhead_recovery_plan.pdf.
3 "Fealty to symbolism is no way to save salmon," in "Effective Conservation Science: Data Not Dogma," by P. Kareiva, and V. Carranza, edited by Peter Kareiva, Michelle Marvier, and Brian Silliman: Oxford University Press, 2018, DOI: 10.1093/oso/9780198808978.003.0015, at http://www.pugetsoundanglers.org/Fealty_to_symbolism_is_no_way_to_save_salmon.pdf.
4 "Southern resident killer whale priority Chinook stocks," NOAA Fisheries and Washington State Department of Fish and Wildlife, June 22, 2018, at https://www.documentcloud.org/documents/4615304-SRKW-Priority-Chinook-Stocks.html.

In their briefing paper on "Southern Resident Killer Whales and Snake River Dams," NOAA Fisheries wrote:

"...the relative size of the Snake River salmon stocks compared to others on the West Coast means that increases in their numbers, whether from breaching dams or otherwise, would result in only a marginal change in the total salmon available to the killer whales."[5]

According to the Army Corps of Engineers, the cost to remove the dams would be more than $1 Billion.[6] A $1 billion public expense would be equal to more than 11 years of state funding for salmon recovery efforts in Western Washington. In the 2019-21 state Capital Budget, funding for six salmon recovery funds amounted to $173.5 million.[7]

Increasing funding for salmon recovery, even by a few million dollars has been politically difficult. It is unclear where politicians would find $1 billion. Encouraging politicians to spend public money on destroying the dams, rather than focusing resources where the science indicates is counterproductive and will end up harming orca recovery.

The high cost of replacing the electricity

The four Lower Snake River Dams provide about seven percent of Washington's electricity, providing about 7.5 million megawatt

---

5 "Southern Resident Killer Whales and Snake River Dams," NOAA Fisheries West Coast Region, 2016, at https://www.westcoast.fisheries.noaa.gov/publications/protected_species/marine_mammals/killer_whales/killerwhales_snakeriverdams.pdf.
6 "Final Feasibility Study and Environmental Impact Statement," U.S. Army Corps of Engineers, Annex X, page D-X-3, 1998.
7 The funds included here are the Salmon Recovery Funding Board, the Puget Sound Acquisition and Restoration Fund, Floodplains by Design, as well as accounts for estuaries, coastal restoration and fish passage.

hours (MWh) of electricity.[8] That is more than the amount generated by all solar panels and wind turbines in Washington state combined.

In 2018, the NW Energy Coalition commissioned a study to argue for dam removal.[9] Their report said it would cost $464 million a year to replace 86 percent of the energy with renewables.

Some activists claim the energy from the dams is not needed at all. The producer of a documentary calling for dam destruction claimed, "If we took those dams out, we would not need to replace the electricity and we would all save money."[10]

The Northwest Power and Conservation Council (NWPCC) warn the Northwest is facing an energy shortage even with the dams. If the dams were removed, the shortage would get worse, and an NWPCC analyst confirmed that "without these dams, LOLP [Loss of Load Probability] increases significantly."

Conclusion

Salmon populations along the Snake River are greater today than two decades ago, and the fish survival rate continues to improve.

To help salmon and orca, Washington policymakers should put funding where it will be most effective. Preserving the Snake

---

8 "Emissions & Generation Resource Integrated Database (eGRID)," U.S. Environmental Protection Agency, February 15, 2018, at https://www.epa.gov/energy/emissions-generation-resource-integrated-database-egrid.
9 "Lower Snake River Dams Power Replacement Study," Northwest Energy Coalition, March 2018, at https://nwenergy.org/wp-content/uploads/2018/04/LSRD_Report_Full_Final.pdf.
10 "Film Finds Momentum for Removing Dams to Save Orcas," by Eric Tegethoff, Public News Service, August 19, 2019, at https://www.publicnewsservice.org/2019-08-16/endangered-species-and-wildlife/film-finds-momentum-for-removing-dams-to-save-orcas/a67462-1.

River dams is not only good for our economy, farmers, and energy – it is good for orcas and the environment.

3. Policy Recommendation: Protect honeybees and farmers with good science

The claims about recent honeybee deaths are dramatic. Environment Washington's web page proclaims, "Millions of bees are dying off, with alarming consequences for our environment and our food supply. ... It's simple: No bees, no food."[11] There has been an increase in the percentage of honeybee hives that die each year, and Environment Washington is not alone in blaming pesticides, climate change or other environmental factors.

These claims, however, ignore the fact that beekeepers have successfully replaced lost hives. Surveys of beekeepers by the U.S. Department of Agriculture (USDA) show that the most serious threat is the varroa mite, which attaches itself to honeybees, spreading disease and shortening their lifespan.

Increase in honeybee mortality

According to the USDA, the percentage of honeybee hives that die annually has increased from about 20 percent twenty years ago, to about 40 percent in four of the last five years.[12] Hobbyist beekeepers have the highest mortality, losing nearly 51 percent of hives in 2017-18. Commercial beekeepers have the lowest level of hive loss, losing 33 percent of hives.[13] The knowledge of beekeepers and the incentive to keep hives alive have a strong influence on hive mortality.

---

11 "No Bees, No Food," Environment Washington, accessed October 3, 2019, at https://environmentwashington.org/programs/wae/no-bees-no-food.
12 "Honey Bee Colony Losses 2018-2019: Preliminary Results," Bee Informed Partnership, June 19, 2019, at https://beeinformed.org/results/2018-2019/.
13 "National Management Survey," Bee Informed Partnership, 2018-2019, at https://bip2.beeinformed.org/survey/.

The number of honeybee hives in the United States has actually increased in recent years. In 2000, the USDA estimates there were about 2.68 million hives in the US.[14] In 2019, the estimate is 2.8 million hives.[15] Far from seeing a decline in the honeybee population, beekeepers have ensured the population is higher than at any time in the last two decades.

Why are bees dying?

It is important to understand why hives are dying, so beekeepers, farmers, and policymakers can address the real problem.

Hobbyist beekeepers have higher mortality rates because they are less likely to have effective strategies to reduce varroa mites. The USDA notes that:

"Many backyard beekeepers don't have any varroa control strategies in place. We think this results in colonies collapsing and spreading mites to neighboring colonies that are otherwise well-managed for mites."[16]

Rather than listening to beekeepers or the USDA reports, politicians blame pesticides, especially a type of pesticide known as neonics. The evidence linking neonics to hive death, however, is flimsy.

Neonics are primarily an agricultural pesticide. Commercial

14 "Honey," National Agricultural Statistics Service, U.S. Department of Agriculture, February 28, 2001, at https://downloads.usda.library.cornell.edu/usda-esmis/files/hd76s004z/vm40xv388/hd76s2432/Hone-02-28-2001.pdf.
15 "Honey, National Agricultural Statistics Service, U.S. Department of Agriculture, May 16, 2019, at https://downloads.usda.library.cornell.edu/usda-esmis/files/hd76s004z/j098zm46r/d504rv45m/hony0519.pdf.
16 "Nation's beekeepers lost 44 percent of bees in 2015-16," Bee Informed Partnership, May 10, 2016, at https://beeinformed.org/2016/05/10/nations-beekeepers-lost-44-percent-of-bees-in-2015-16/.

beekeepers, those with the greatest exposure to agricultural pesticides, have the lowest rates of mortality. Only 13.6 percent of beekeepers named pesticides of all kinds as a "stressor" during the first quarter of 2019. By way of comparison, 45.6 percent named varroa mites.[17]

Studies for the prevalence of neonics in hives finds very low levels. USDA found only 1.9 percent of pollen found in hives tested positive for a common neonic known as *imidacloprid,* and only 1.2 percent tested positive for *clothianidin.*[18] Many beekeepers worry that neonics will be replaced with more harmful pesticides. Scientist and beekeeper Randy Oliver argues:

"Instead of putting unwarranted lobbying effort against the single insecticide clothianidin, the bee industry would better benefit by going after … 'the low-hanging fruit'—the all-too-common bee kills due to spray applications of other pesticides."[19]

Another claim is that climate change is harming bees. This is a strange claim. Honeybees are believed to have originated in Africa and are not native to the United States. There were 530,000 hives in North Dakota in 2018, and 335,000 hives in California, representing the top two states for the number of hives. These states have two very different climates, and honeybees thrive in both.[20]

---

17 "Honey Bee Colonies," National Agricultural Statistics Service, U.S. Department of Agriculture, August 1, 2019, at https://downloads.usda.library. cornell.edu/usda-esmis/files/rn301137d/f7623q868/ft849239n/hcny0819.pdf.
18 "National Honey bee Survey Pesticide Report, 2011 to 2019" Bee Informed Partnership, accessed October 3, 2019, at https://bip2.beeinformed.org/state_ reports/pesticides/
19 "Neonicitinoids: Trying to make sense of the science, Part 2," by Randy Oliver, September 2012, American Bee Journal (ABJ), Scientificbeekeeping. com, at http://scientificbeekeeping.com/neonicotinoids-trying-to-make-sense-of-the-science-part-2/.
20 NASS, U.S. Department of Agriculture, 2019.

Beekeepers and farmers are protecting honeybee populations

Beekeepers and farmers have strong incentives to keep honeybee populations strong. Farmers pay for pollination services, and beekeepers lose income for every hive lost. Although beekeepers have not yet successfully reduced annual mortality, they have compensated by replacing hives faster than they are being lost. Free markets have saved the bees.

Conclusion

The risks to honeybees continue, but blaming pesticides needlessly pits farmers and beekeepers against each other and risks bringing back older pesticides that are more toxic to bees.

4. Policy Recommendation: Require environmental spending to meet effectiveness benchmarks

Using regulation and direct subsidies, Washington state is spending a significant amount to reduce CO_2 emissions in the state. The justification is that we face a "climate crisis." Despite that rhetoric, the state does nothing to ensure taxpayer funds are spent to achieve the most CO_2 reduction for every dollar.

Whether climate change is a crisis or a manageable risk, lawmakers should adopt performance standards for climate-related policy and regulation. Such standards not only represent the responsible use of taxpayer funds but are environmentally responsible. If activists believe we face a climate crisis, they should be the most vocal demanding that the action we take is effective.

High cost, poor results

The market provides good metrics for the price of effective CO_2

reduction. In 2019, the average market price for reduce one metric ton (MT) of CO_2e[21] ranges from about $17 in California's cap-and-trade system[22] to seven dollars paid by Seattle City Light.[23] Individuals can invest in certified CO2 reduction projects for about $10/MT from places like Bonneville Environmental Foundation.[24] The price of Washington state climate policy far exceeds these costs.

For example, starting in 2007, the management consultant McKinsey published its "greenhouse gas abatement cost curves," ranking the most cost-effective approaches to reducing CO2 emissions.[25] The prioritization approach has been recognized as the most effective approach to maximizing the effectiveness of CO2 policy and was referenced by Governor Inslee's first climate legislation in 2013.[26] Unfortunately, Washington state elected officials and agency staff have not followed this approach, instead choosing projects that have high costs but yield small CO2 reductions.

Three 2019 policies demonstrate the ineffectiveness of our

---

21 CO2e includes not only CO2 but other greenhouse gases like methane and sulfur hexafluoride.

22 "California cap-and-trade program," California Air Resources Board, August 2019, at https://ww3.arb.ca.gov/cc/capandtrade/auction/results_summary.pdf.

23 Author interview with Oradona Landgrebe, Environmental Affairs, Seattle City Light, August 22, 2019.

24 "Carbon offset projects," Projects and Programs, Bonneville Environmental Foundation, accessed October 4, 2019, at http://www.b-e-f.org/environmental-projects-and-programs/carbon-offset-projects/all/.

25 "Pathways to a low-carbon economy: Version 2 of the global greenhouse gas abatement cost curve," McKinsey and Company, September 2013, at https://www.mckinsey.com/business-functions/sustainability/our-insights/pathways-to-a-low-carbon-economy.

26 "Evaluation of Approaches to Reduce Greenhouse Gas Emissions in Washington State – Final Report," prepared for State of Washington Climate Legislative and Executive Working Group (CLEW), Leidos, October 14, 2013, at http://www.governor.wa.gov/sites/default/files/documents/Task_4_Final_Report_10-13-2013.pdf.

current approach. First, the legislature adopted a requirement that 100 percent of Washington's electricity be CO2-free by 2045. Analysis by the Low Carbon Prosperity Institute found that the approach will cost between $60 and $90 per MT of CO2 reduced.[27]

Second, the Washington State Department of Ecology provided $13.3 million to counties for electric buses. Based on the anticipated lifespan of the buses, it costs about $195 for every metric ton of CO2 avoided.[28]

Third, the legislature reinstated subsidies for electric vehicle buyers. These subsidies are extremely ineffective, costing about $158 to reduce one MT of CO2.[29] If the state followed the lead of Seattle City Light and invested in CO2 reduction projects available on the market, it would reduce nearly 28 times as much CO2.

One reason projects are so ineffective is that they are chosen based on politics. As climate researchers Michael Vandenbergh and Jonathan Gilligan note in their book, the government often "requires other goals to be achieved" unrelated to CO2 reduction.[30] Rather than address the "climate crisis," politicians reward special interest groups.

---

27 "Analysis of 100% Clean Bill (SB 5116) Cost Cap," by Kevin Tempest, Low Carbon Prosperity Institute, March 27, 2019, at https://www.lowcarbonprosperity.org/2019/03/27/analysis-of-100-clean-bill-sb-5116-cost-cap/.
28 "How Washington's new electric bus is like a $616 latte," by Todd Myers, Washington Policy Center, June 18, 2019, at https://www.washingtonpolicy.org/publications/detail/how-washingtons-new-electric-bus-is-like-a-616-latte.
29 "Tax breaks for wealthy electric vehicle buyers won't reduce CO2 emissions," by Todd Myers, Washington Policy Center, February 28, 2019, at https://www.washingtonpolicy.org/publications/detail/tax-breaks-for-wealthy-electric-vehicle-buyers-wont-reduce-co2-emissions.
30 "Beyond Politics: The Private Governance Response to Climate Change," by Michael Vandenbergh and Jonathan Gilligan, Cambridge University Press, 2017, page 250.

Set standards for effectiveness

Legislators should adopt metrics of effectiveness for all climate policy to ensure we maximize CO_2 reduction. First, Washington state should not spend more than $20 per metric ton of CO_2.

Second, all state funds related to reducing CO_2, including subsidies for electric vehicles, renewable energy and the Clean Energy Fund, should instead be used to invest in CO_2-reduction projects on the open market. These policies are appropriate no matter how large or small the risk from climate change is.

Conclusion

Washington could do more to reduce CO_2 emissions and mitigate the impact of climate change by setting some basic standards and following a trend that has been recognized as the gold standard for more than a decade.

5. Policy Recommendation: Three steps to help salmon in the near term

When the Puget Sound Partnership (PSP) was created in 2007, it set a target to "Stop the overall decline and start seeing improvements in wild Chinook abundance" by 2020.[31] Populations, however, have not recovered, and progress toward this goal has been slow.

The real work to recover salmon will take time and rely on incremental improvements. With the need to increase salmon populations in the near term, legislators should prioritize projects that help salmon today.

---

31 "Chinook Salmon Population Abundance," Puget Sound Vital Sign, Puget Sound Partnership, July 11, 2019, at https://vitalsigns.pugetsoundinfo.wa.gov/ VitalSignIndicator/Detail/4.

Salmon populations are not increasing

This year, PSP updated its assessment of Chinook recovery, noting the population is "not improving," and is below the 2020 target. They noted, "None of the populations of Puget Sound Chinook salmon are currently meeting recovery goals for abundance of natural-origin spawners."

Three salmon recovery strategies

1. Reduce competition from seals and sea lions

Seal and sea lion populations have increased, and they are eating Chinook salmon that could be available as a food source for orca. A 2018 study found "significant negative correlations between seal densities and productivity of Chinook salmon for 14 of 20 wild Chinook populations in the Pacific Northwest."[32]

A law to amend the Marine Mammal Protection Act and allow states and Indian tribes to kill predatory sea lions at the mouth of the Columbia River passed Congress with bipartisan support in 2018.[33] Expanding the authority to reduce populations elsewhere would immediately increase prey availability for Puget Sound orca.

2. Increase hatchery production

Hatchery production has steadily declined for more than two decades. Puget Sound hatchery production has fallen from about 110 million in the late 1990s, down to under 80 million in 2017. In

---

32 "Wild Chinook salmon productivity is negatively related to seal density and not related to hatchery releases in the Pacific Northwest," by Benjamin W. Nelson, Carl J. Walters, Andrew W. Trites, and Murdoch K. McAllister, Canadian Journal of Fisheries and Aquatic Sciences, 2019, 76(3), pages 447-462, at https://doi.org/10.1139/cjfas-2017-0481.

33 "House passes bill to cull predatory Columbia River sea lions," by George Plaven, Capital Press, June 28, 2018, at https://www.capitalpress.com/nation_world/ap_nation_world/house-passes-bill-to-cull-predatory-columbia-river-sea-lions/article_359dcccc-8b82-5f73-85ec-1e07bf2709c2.html.

some watersheds, like the Elwha River on the Olympic Peninsula, where hatchery fish represent 96 percent of all salmon, hatcheries are critical to maintaining viable populations.[34]

The legislature increased funding for hatcheries in the 2019-21 state budget, which is encouraging. Although it takes several years for hatchery fish to return and become available to orca and sport and tribal fishers, the timeline is shorter than other approaches.

3. Make farmers partners in habitat recovery

Farmland can play an important part in salmon recovery. Too often, however, the financial burden of salmon recovery on farmland is placed on the farmer. Costs should be borne by everyone, not just farmers providing ecosystem services that city-dwellers cannot.

The work of conservation districts and the Conservation Reserve Enhancement Program (CREP) are important parts of the effort to reward farmers who create salmon habitat while maintaining a variable farm.[35] Several improvements, however, are necessary.

The legislature should fund pilot projects that provide incentives to match that value in a one-time incentive that provides equivalent net income for producers of high-value crops such as cranberries, blueberries and orchards. Lawmakers should offer a cumulative impact incentive to reward agricultural producers who enroll 50% of farmland along a stream with a one-time bonus.

---

34 "Age Structure and Hatchery Fraction of Elwha River Chinook Salmon: 2017 Carcass Survey Report," by Josh Weinheimer, Joseph Anderson, Randy Cooper, Scott Williams, Mike McHenry, Patrick Crain, Sam Brenkman, and Heidi Hugunin, Washington State Department of Fish and Wildlife Fish Program Science Division, FPA 18-05, June 2018.
35 "Conservation Reserve Enhancement Program (CREP)," Washington State Conservation Commission, at https://scc.wa.gov/crep/.

Conclusion

In the near term, we need to take steps that can produce increases in the next few years. Reducing predation, increasing hatchery production, and making farmers partners will offer near-term environmental improvements until longer-term efforts begin to show results.

6. Policy Recommendation: The wasteful ineffectiveness of a low-carbon fuel standard

Transportation accounts for the largest portion of Washington's CO_2 emissions, accounting for about 40% of the total, so, policymakers have focused on reducing transportation emissions. The key, however, is to reduce CO_2 emissions in ways that are effective.

A low-carbon fuel standard (LCFS) is an expensive way to reduce CO_2 emissions and air pollution. It is also extremely ineffective at reducing traditional forms of air pollution, like particulate matter.

High cost to reduce CO_2

The primary justification for the LCFS is that it reduces the carbon intensity of transportation fuels. The legislation previously offered in Olympia sets a goal to reduce the carbon intensity of gasoline by 20 percent by 2035.

Ultimately, the costs to meet those goals are borne by drivers. We have a good idea of what those costs will be based on real-world experience in California and Oregon.

In California, the price to reduce one MT of CO_2 has hovered around $190 since early 2018. That price translates to about 34 cents per gallon when the LCFS reaches its goal of reducing the carbon intensity of gasoline by 20 percent. In Oregon, the price doubled from 2018 to mid-2019, when the credit price for one MT of CO_2 jumped to $156.20.[36]

These prices are extremely high. The Bonneville Environmental Foundation offers projects that reduce one MT of CO_2 for $10.[37] Seattle City Light, which invests in projects that reduce CO_2 emissions to offset emissions from electricity generated by natural gas, pays about seven dollars per MT of CO_2 avoided.[38]

No reduction in particulate matter

The advocates of the LCFS in Washington state argue it will also reduce particulate matter (PM). The Department of Ecology found the LCFS would reduce PM 2.5 by about one percent ten years after it was implemented.[39]

Some argue that an LCFS would benefit communities near roads that may be more exposed to PM from cars. The claim is that an LCFS would reduce asthma and other illnesses. No data, however, has been offered to back up this claim.

---

36 "Monthly CFP Credit Transfer Report for July 2019," Oregon Department of Environmental Quality, August 6, 2019, at https://www.oregon.gov/deq/ FilterDocs/CFPCreditTransferActivityReport.xlsx. The measurement refers to airborne particles 2.5 microns in size.
37 "Carbon offset project portfolio," Projects and Programs, Bonneville Environmental Foundation, accessed October 4, 2019, at http://www.b-e-f.org/ environmental-projects-and-programs/carbon-offset-projects/all/
38 Author interview with Oradona Landgrebe, Environmental Affairs, Seattle City Light, August 22, 2019.
39 "A Clean Fuel Standard in Washington State: Revised Analysis with Updated Assumptions," by Jennifer Pont, Stefan Unnasch, et al., Final Report, LCA 8056.98.2014, Life Cycle Associates LLC, December 12, 2014, at https://www. ofm.wa.gov/sites/default/files/public/legacy/reports/Carbon_Fuel_Standard_ evaluation_2014_final.pdf.

The market alternative to an LCFS

Support for a low-carbon fuel standard is based on the argument that Washington must reduce transportation-related CO2 emissions. The goal should be to provide the greatest CO2 reduction for the least cost. An LCFS fails that test.

To effectively reduce CO2 emissions, the state should follow the lead of Seattle City Light and others who invest in carbon reduction projects on the market. Many organizations offer projects that have been independently certified to be effective by organizations like Green-e.[40] According to state estimates, implementing the low-carbon fuel standard would cost about $750,000 per year.[41] At the rate paid by Seattle City Light – about seven dollars per MT of CO2 – that would remove the CO2 from nearly 27,000 cars annually.

Conclusion

If Washington state or other jurisdictions adopt an LCFS rule, lawmakers should allow the use of certified CO2 reductions to meet the requirements of the rule. This would cut the cost by about 95 percent while achieving the same CO2 reduction goals.

Among the many strategies to reduce CO2 emissions, a low-carbon fuel standard is one of the most expensive and least effective. Washington should reject this approach, which is bad for the economy and the environment.

---

40 "A global third-party certification program for carbon offsets," Certified products and companies, Green-e Climate, accessed October 4, 2019, at https://www.green-e.org/programs/climate.

41 "Multiple Agency Fiscal Note Summary: SB 5412, Greenhouse gases, transportation fuels," Office of Financial Management, Washington State Legislature, January 30, 2019, at https://fortress.wa.gov/FNSPublicSearch/GetPDF?packageID=53932. Fiscal Note shows two-year cost of $1.5 million.

Additional resources

"The costs and impacts of three carbon tax bills," by Todd Myers, Legislative Memo, Washington Policy Center, April 2019

"The false promises and high cost of the low-carbon fuel mandate," by Todd Myers, Washington Policy Center, April 23, 2019

"With billions more in the state budget, it's time to fully fund salmon recovery," by Todd Myers, guest editorial, *The Seattle Times*, April 11, 2019

The high environmental cost of proposed 2019 climate legislation, by Todd Myers, Washington Policy Center, April 8, 2019

"Scientific priorities (not Marx) should guide orca recovery," by Todd Myers, Washington Policy Center, February 4, 2019

"Could removing Snake River dams increase fish kill?" by Todd Myers, Washington Policy Center, December 18, 2018

"How smartphones can reduce our carbon footprint," by Todd Myers, TED Talk San Juan Islands, Washington Policy Center, January 31, 2018

"The Environmental trade-offs of removing the Snake River dams, by Todd Myers, Idaho Law Review, Volume 53, 2017, pages 209-238

"Beekeepers agree: The biggest threat to honeybees isn't pesticides," by Todd Myers, Washington Policy Center, May 18, 2017

"Is climate change killing honeybees?" by Todd Myers, Washington Policy Center, June 24, 2014

CHAPTER FOUR
IMPROVING HEALTH CARE COVERAGE

1. Policy Recommendation: Repeal the state public option to increase health care affordability and choice

More than half of Washington residents, 52% or 3.8 million people, receive health care coverage through their employer or their spouse's employer.[1] Employer-based coverage in the private market is popular, and most people want this coverage to continue.

A further 1.3 million residents are enrolled in the state Medicare entitlement program for the elderly, with annual public spending of about $12.6 billion.[2]

The Medicaid entitlement was originally intended as a safety-net program for the poor, yet today fully 25% of the state population, or 1.8 million Washingtonians, have been put into the program, for a further annual cost of $12 billion. The poverty rate in Washington is only 11%.[3]

About 220,000 people have individual coverage through

1 "Health insurance coverage of the total population," State Health Facts, Washington state, Kaiser Family Foundation, 2017, at https://www.kff.org/other/state-indicator/total-population/?currentTimeframe=0&sortModel=%7B%22colId%22:%22Location%22,%22sort%22:%22asc%22%7D.

2 Total number of Medicare beneficiaries," State Health Facts, Washington state, Kaiser Family Foundation, 2018, https://www.kff.org/medicare/state-indicator/total-medicare-beneficiaries/?currentTimeframe=0&sortModel=%7B%22colId%22:%22Location%22,%22sort%22:%22asc%22%7D.

3 "Washington percent of population in poverty, 1969-2017," Population in Poverty, Washington Data and Research, Office of Financial Management, last modified May 21, 2019, at https://www.ofm.wa.gov/washington-data-research/statewide-data/washington-trends/social-economic-conditions/population-poverty. The figure includes children enrolled in the state Children's Health Insurance Program (CHIP), which is funded through Medicaid.

Washington's subsidized Obamacare exchange, and a further 108,000 people have individual coverage in the free market.[4] The uninsured rate in Washington is 5.5 percent or about 400,000 people.[5]

Restricting patient choice – the state public option plan

The Washington legislature recently passed the country's first public option health plan, which will be administered through the Washington State Health Benefit Exchange.

The public option is a government-subsidized health plan designed to compete against private insurance in the individual and small group markets. The plan will be offered to any one earning up to 500 percent of the federal poverty level. For a family of four, that is an income of $129,000 a year in 2019, a level of about twice the average working family wage in the state.

Obviously, this is not a social safety-net program; it is intended an incremental step toward imposing a single-payer, socialized health care system. The public option plan is designed to include the following: reduced deductibles, more services before the deductible is paid, predictable cost sharing, more government

---

4 "Washington's health insurance marketplace: history and news of the state's exchange," by Louise Morris, Health insurance and health reform authority, Health Insurance.org, May 20, 2019, at https://www.healthinsurance.org/washington-state-health-insurance-exchange/, and "Data Note: Changes in enrollment in the individual health insurance market through early 2019," by Rachel Fehr, Cynthia Cox and Larry Levitt, Kaiser Family Foundation, August 21, 2019, at https://www.kff.org/private-insurance/issue-brief/data-note-changes-in-enrollment-in-the-individual-health-insurance-market-through-early-2019/.
5 "After a three year decline, Washington's uninsured rates shows no change in 2017," by Wei Yen and Thea Mounts, Research Brief No. 89, Washington State Health Research Project, Office of Financial Management, December 2018, at https://www.ofm.wa.gov/sites/default/files/public/dataresearch/researchbriefs/brief089.pdf.

subsidies, a limit on cost sharing to 10 percent of an enrollee's yearly income, and a limit on increase in premium rates.

Public option plan is government-defined and directed

Beginning in 2025, all plans in the state exchange must be standardized. The standardized plans would cut payments to doctors and hospitals to match federal Medicare rates (Medicare payments average 30 percent less than what private insurance pays). Private insurance companies manage the plan under the direction of the Insurance Commissioner. In other words, plan services and payments are limited and defined by the government.

The real cost of the program is to federal taxpayers. The Obamacare exchanges are in a death spiral because of adverse selection. Young, healthy individuals are not participating because they do not want or need all of the government-mandated benefits. The higher costs leaves older and sicker people in the state exchanges.

The premium subsidies in the public option plans will be much higher than in the standard Obamacare exchange plans, placing a much higher tax burden on federal taxpayers. Of course, federal taxpayers are state taxpayers, so ultimately, the tax burden will wind up on Washingtonians.

Private plans can't compete against government subsidies

It is impossible for private citizens to compete against the government. For example, Medicare devastated the thriving private health insurance market for seniors. The public option, once up and running, will have the same effect on the individual and small group health insurance markets in Washington state. As private choices fade, employers may even discontinue employee health benefits, which will increase the government-reach into our health care.

The public option is designed as an incremental move toward a single-payer, government-controlled health care system for the state and the country.

Conclusion

Lawmakers should repeal Washington state's public option law to allow greater choices, competition and affordability in the private market, so employers and families can select the price and level of coverage that best fit their needs.

2. Policy Recommendation: Avoid imposing a socialized single-payer system

The Affordable Care Act (ACA), also known as Obamacare, was enacted in 2010. It is a highly complex law that has made our current health care delivery system more costly and confusing. In comparison, a socialized single-payer system is attractive to many people because of its perceived simplicity – the U.S. government would direct health services for all Americans.

Problems with the Canadian system

Canada has had a single-payer system for over 30 years, and its hard experiences are revealing. Canadians are proud of the idea that every citizen has health insurance, at least in theory. From a cultural identity standpoint, the principle of universal coverage is a priority for the country. National pride in the broad idea also makes it easier for the citizens to overlook the many problems they experience in the system.

Perceived as "free," the demand for health care far outweighs the supply of care. All industrialized countries face the same age demographic problem, whereby the younger, working-age group is getting smaller, while the older, non-working group is getting larger in proportion to the total population. Financing for a single-payer socialized system is pay-as-you-go – there is no long-term trust fund, only monthly taxes paid by workers. This aging demographic imbalance guarantees a looming financial disaster in Canadian health care funding in the future.

Using waiting lists to ration health care

The long waiting times in a single-payer system are not in the patient's best interest and would not be acceptable for the vast majority of Americans. Health care rationing through waiting lists happens when supply is overwhelmed by demand. The question is whether government bureaucrats should have the authority to pick and choose what medical procedures patients receive and who should actually receive those treatments, while others, usually older, sicker patients, are forced to wait for care.

Conclusion

A single-payer system discourages innovation. There is virtually no money in the system to encourage investment in new life-saving medicines and medical devices. Lack of innovation guarantees that under single-payer few new treatments would be discovered, with little or no improvement in quality of life or life expectancy, particularly for the medically vulnerable and the elderly.

Further politicizing health care services

Under a single-payer system, health care spending must compete with all other government activity and political interests for funding. This makes health care very political and subject to change with every new budget. It also forces each health care sector, for example, hospitals and doctors, to compete with each other for limited public money.

No government bureaucrat is more concerned about a person's health than that person is. Patients, as health care consumers, should be allowed to be informed about, to review the prices of, and to gain access to the best health care services available in a fair, open, and free marketplace.

As the real-world examples of Canada and the failures of the U.S. Veterans Administration hospital system show, a single-payer system does none of these things, leaving patients at the mercy of a distant, bureaucratic and heavily politicized health care system.

3. Policy Recommendation: Do not use other countries as a model for U.S. health care

The United States has a complex health care delivery system composed of private and government-funded insurance plans. Half of all Americans receive their health insurance from their employer or their spouse's employer. Over forty percent of Americans receive their health insurance from the government. The remainder are either uninsured or obtain health insurance through the private individual market. The current political debate concerns how large a role the government should play in our health care delivery system.

The United States spends far more money per-person on health care than other industrialized countries. Last year, overall medical spending in the U.S. totaled $3.5 trillion or 18 percent of the national gross domestic product.

Other countries devote fewer resources to health care

Because other countries spend less on health care, they are often promoted as useful models for the U.S. However, looking to other countries to solve our health care delivery system problems is not practical or reasonable. Most other countries are smaller than the U.S., have a more homogenous population and have lower rates of immigration and diversity. What the people of one country favor may not be applicable or acceptable to people living in a different society.

One fact does remain, though. In all other industrialized countries, the demand for health care is much greater than the money politicians' budget to pay for it. The results of this supply/demand mismatch are chronic shortages, followed by strict rationing of health care. The rationing can take many forms – from long waits to denying the elderly access to certain procedures, to allowing individuals with political influence to receive priority attention from providers.

As noted, Canada uses waiting lists to ration care. In 2018, waiting times for specialty care averaged 20 weeks. Canada actually has a two-tiered system, socialized services in the country, and travel to the U.S. for privately-funded care.

Great Britain enacted a government system in 1948, the National Health Service, to give every citizen cradle-to-grave coverage. About ten percent of the population has private insurance and many physicians combine government-paid work with private practice. In 2018, 250,000 citizens waited more than six months for needed treatments within the NHS, while 36,000 British waited nine months or more.

Using choice to hold down costs

Switzerland has a comparatively large private health care sector, and patients are responsible for 30 percent of their own health care costs. Consequently, a certain degree of consumer choice exists in Switzerland and the country has been fairly successful in holding down costs. Unfortunately, as officials increase the number of benefit mandates imposed on insurance plans, health care costs rise.

Singapore has a multi-tiered system with different levels of care, depending on the patient's ability and willingness to pay more. This is similar to the system in the U.S. before Medicare and Medicaid, when competition-controlled costs and private hospitals and doctors treated paying patients and charity hospitals and residents-in-training cared for indigent patients.

Although the overall systems vary, the common factor for all other countries is government-mandated health insurance. Even those countries that have a component of "private" health care continue to mandate that every citizen have government-approved health insurance.

The free market and consumer choice offer the best solution

Politicians push for "universal health coverage," but the critical point is to use the best mechanism to allow the greatest number of Americans access to affordable health care. Simply having health coverage in theory in no way guarantees timely access to actual care. The American experience with the Veterans Administration hospital system, a government-run, single-payer health care program, reveals unacceptable waiting times and huge inefficiencies.

Just like all other economic activities, the free market offers the best solution to provide the greatest access to health care and to control costs. People freely making their own health care decisions and using their own health care dollars would give Americans the best chance to utilize their right to access health care, with tax-funded safety-net health programs provided for those who can't afford it.

4. Policy Recommendation: Promote structural reforms at the state level, free of federal government restrictions

States can enact their own health care reform, regardless of federal actions, that would increase access to health care while decreasing costs. Here is a list of policy options available to state policymakers under current federal law:

1. Request 1332 and 1115A waivers. Under these two sections, states can request, and the Administration can approve, significant changes in the implementation of the ACA without action by Congress.

2. Pass state legislation to limit state taxpayers' contribution to the Medicaid expansion. States can opt-out of costly Medicaid expansion under the ACA, freeing resources that can be used for state-level health programs.

3. Repeal Certificate of Need laws. Research now shows that state Certificate of Need rules do not lower costs, but that they do limit patient choices by banning investment and construction of new health care facilities.

4. Enact legal reform to reduce wasteful medical expenses. Legal fees and defensive medicine (ordering unneeded tests) add tremendously to health care costs, without increasing patient choices or quality of care.

5. Cut state mandates on health care services. Each mandate adds to the cost of health insurance and, while catering to politically-connected special interest groups, often reduces choices for patients. Legislatures should repeal most of their state-imposed health insurance mandates.

6. Expand and promote the use of association health plans. Association health plans allow small groups to join together to purchase health insurance in the same way large groups do. Large group plans are regulated by the federal ERISA law and therefore avoid many of the worst features of the ACA.

7. Promote telemedicine. Telemedicine and similar online services reduce costs and increase patient access to health care, especially for people living in rural areas.

8. Eliminate or decrease waste, fraud, and abuse in the Medicaid program. A high percentage of Medicaid costs do not increase care or access for enrollees. The massive bureaucratic nature of the program makes it a target for cheating and financial crime.

9. Encourage home health care in Medicaid. Costs are less and patient satisfaction is higher with home health care. It reduces government involvement in care and respects the supportive family relationships of patients.

10. Cap Medicaid enrollment. Congress originally intended Medicaid to be targeted to help the most vulnerable patients while encouraging well-off patients to buy affordable private health insurance coverage.

11. Reduce restrictive licensing laws. States should cut barriers to medical practice to increase access to skilled health care services for patients.

12. Encourage direct primary care. For a fixed amount per month, patients can access primary care without waiting. Direct primary care increases access to doctors for all patients, regardless of income. Legislatures should encourage direct primary care and protect doctors from state regulatory insurance laws.

Lawmakers should enact deep structural reforms like these to promote innovation in the health care market, attract talented medical professionals, and increase access and lower costs for patients.

5. Policy Recommendation: Focus illegal drug enforcement on dealers and suppliers

The 50-year fight against illegal drugs has cost taxpayers over one trillion dollars and yet has been of limited effectiveness. The drug crisis in the United States continues, and a different approach is needed.

When considering the current opioid crisis, focusing punishment on prescription drug manufacturers and doctors is misplaced. Data from the government Center for Disease Control confirm that the alarming increase in opioid deaths over the past ten years is from illicit fentanyl and heroin, not legally-available medications.

Any market transaction depends on the supply of a product or service and the demand for that product or service. The illegal drug trade is no different. For a war on drugs to be successful, it must reduce both the supply and the demand for drugs.

Drug abuse as a treatable disease

One key strategy is to treat drug abuse as a treatable disease, just like many cases of mental illness. Advocates of this viewpoint support more money for treatment and prevention, rather than money for police activity. To date, law enforcement has accounted for 75 percent of the money spent on the war on drugs.

Many who view drug abuse as a disease would like to see less enforcement against the drug user and more emphasis on prosecuting major suppliers and manufacturers of illegal drugs. This is not to be confused with the legalization of all drugs.

The incarceration of the user is extremely expensive for taxpayers and provides no real treatment or long-term solution. Shifting resources to prosecuting suppliers while providing treatment for users is a constructive approach and is not an argument for legalization.

Providing needed pain relief

An unintended consequence of the current opioid crisis is that patients who are truly in pain are often denied the level of prescription pain relief they actually need. This limitation is obviously a disservice to thousands of patients living in pain who could benefit from opioid medications, and whose monitored use of pain medicine is not contributing to the opioid crisis.

Doctors are able to assess and treat a patient's pain in the most timely fashion. They should not be restricted by arbitrary laws that limit how much pain relief they can provide.

6. Policy Recommendation: Enact reforms to strengthen the Medicare entitlement

The federal Medicare and Medicaid entitlement programs are over 50 years old. They have become two of the largest health insurance plans in the country and account for an ever-increasing share of federal and state spending.

In the coming decades, they will also require more public spending than any government program and will become financially unsustainable unless they are restructured and reformed. The survival of Medicare and Medicaid depends on patient-oriented reforms that must occur sooner rather than later to protect vital health services for patients.

Modernizing Medicare

From the start, the cost of the Medicare program was badly underestimated. The Administration promised Congress in 1965 that the funding would require much less than one percent of payroll taxes. By the late 1980s, however, this was increased to 1.6 percent and subsequently to 2.9 percent.

In inflation-adjusted dollars, spending on Medicare was $4.6 billion in 1967 but had increased to $7.9 billion by 1971. This was a 70 percent increase, whereas enrollment had increased only six percent. By 1990, Medicare was nine times over its original budget.

There is broad agreement that Medicare is not financially sustainable. The program's costs are rising, the number of workers paying monthly taxes into the program is proportionately decreasing and the number of elderly recipients is dramatically increasing as the post-war generation reaches age 65.

We now have an entire generation of people that have grown up with Medicare, have paid into it and now expect full medical services in return. We also have people in younger generations who understand the bankrupt nature of the program and do not believe Medicare will still exist when they reach age 65.

A fair solution

A fair and workable solution must account for the reasonable expectations of both of these generations and provide reliable health coverage for future generations. As a country, we have a moral obligation to seniors already enrolled in the program and to those approaching retirement age.

A simple first step to Medicare reform would be to raise the age of eligibility gradually. When the program started in 1965, the average life expectancy in the U.S. was 67 years for men and 74 years for women. Average life expectancy is now 76 years for men and 81 years for women, straining an entitlement program beyond what it was designed to support.

Another simple Medicare reform would be more thorough means-testing, not just in Part B. Wealthier seniors would pay more, and low-income people would pay less.

Revive private market choice

As it stands now, there is, understandably, no private insurance market for seniors. Any private market was destroyed by Medicare long ago. It is impossible to compete against the government, which has monopoly power to fix prices and lose money while private insurers go out of business.

Lawmakers should revive the private market for the elderly by allowing people to leave Medicare voluntarily and buy tax-favored health savings accounts and low-cost health plans. Low-income seniors could use subsidized premium support that would allow them to purchase health insurance in the private market, empowering them to make their own choices.

Protecting Medicare doctors

Lawmakers should ensure that Medicare doctors are protected from unfair sanctions or government penalties when they seek partial payments from patients or their insurance companies, instead of being expelled from the program and legally prosecuted as they are now. Doctors should never be forced to choose between caring for their Medicare patients and receiving fair compensation for their work.

Conclusion

Lawmakers should allow future generations to continue the individual health insurance they had during their working life in retirement. As the younger generation saves, their health insurance nest eggs would build until they need it in their later years.

This is the same strategy that millions of individuals and families use today to save for retirement. The federal government informs people that they cannot rely only on Social Security to support them after age 67 and that all working people need to plan for the expected living expenses they will incur later on. The same should be true of Medicare regarding future health care costs.

7. Policy Recommendation: Enact reforms to modernize and strengthen Medicaid

There are currently four groups of people receiving assistance through the Medicaid program. These are the poor, the disabled, low-income mothers and children and individuals needing long-term care. Although mothers and children make up most of the beneficiaries, long-term care accounts for 70 percent of Medicaid's cost.

Fastest-growing state budget cost

Medicaid expenditures are the fastest-growing budget item for virtually all states, even though the federal government supplies, on average, 57 percent of all Medicaid dollars spent in the legacy program and at least 90 percent of dollars in the new ACA-expanded Medicaid program.

In Washington state, Medicaid spending has grown rapidly and now consumes a significant share of the biennial budget. State Medicaid spending rose 44%, from 7.5 billion to nearly $11 billion, from 2012 to 2016.[6]

State reimbursement by the federal government for the traditional Medicaid is based on the wealth of the state, with

6 "Medicaid Spending in Washington," Public Policy in Washington, Ballotpedia (based on data from State Health Facts, Washington state, Kaiser Family Foundation), accessed September 2019, at https://ballotpedia.org/ Medicaid_spending_in_Washington#cite_note-28.

poorer states receiving a higher percentage match of federal money than wealthier ones.

The first step to reform

The most important first step to reforming the federal Medicaid program is to redesign it so it no longer functions as an unsustainable, open-ended entitlement. Welfare reform in the late 1990s was successful because it placed limits on how many years people could expect to receive taxpayer support. Medicaid recipients should have a co-pay requirement based on income and ability to pay.

Where applicable, able-bodied Medicaid enrollees should have a work requirement. Like welfare, Medicaid should be viewed not as a permanent lifestyle, but as a transition to help low-income families achieve self-confidence, economic independence, and full self-sufficiency.

Promoting healthy lifestyles

It is condescending to believe poor families cannot manage their own health care. Allowing them to control their own health care dollars through subsidized health savings accounts or premium vouchers would financially reward enrollees for leading a healthy lifestyle and making smart personal choices. It would also show respect for low-income families, allowing them to be treated equally with others in the community.

Respecting local control

Local control of the management and financing of entitlement programs works best. States, rather than the federal government, should be placed in charge of administering Medicaid. Block grants and waivers from the federal government would allow states to experiment with program designs that work best for their residents and to budget for Medicaid spending more efficiently.

Lawmakers should restore the income requirement to 133 percent of the federal poverty level, so that the neediest families are assured of receiving support. Medicaid should not be a subsidized "safety-net" for middle-income people by encouraging those who can live independently to become dependent for their health care on a tax-subsidized entitlement program.

Additional resources

"Do socialized health care systems in other countries offer a model for the United States?" by Dr. Roger Stark, Policy Brief, Washington Policy Center, July 2019

"Washington state's tax-subsidized public option is designed as a step toward imposing socialized single-payer health care," by Dr. Roger Stark, Policy Notes, Washington Policy Center, June 2019

"Federal administrative improvements to the Affordable Care Act and state options for health care reform," by Dr. Roger Stark, Legislative Memo, Washington Policy Center, January 2018

"A new approach is needed to solve the opioid crisis," by Dr. Roger Stark, Policy Brief, Washington Policy Center, July 2018

"Is a single-payer health care system right for America?" by Dr. Roger Stark, Policy Notes, Washington Policy Center, May 2017

"Medicare and Medicaid at Fifty," by Dr. Roger Stark, Policy Notes, Washington Policy Center, September 2015

CHAPTER FIVE
IMPROVING PUBLIC SCHOOLS

1. Policy recommendation: Recognize that Washington schools receive ample funding

In 2017, state lawmakers of both parties joined together and passed a historic bill to provide schools with the greatest funding increase in Washington state history. This bill, HB 2242, was the legislature's final resolution of the state supreme court's 2012 *McCleary* decision, and the latest in a series of six years of higher taxes and more funding to schools.

In June 2018, the court signaled approval of the bill and ended the *McCleary* case. The Washington state legislature has thus met the constitutional standard of "ample funding" for education, and today every public school across the state receives more money than ever before.

Public school spending has doubled in eight years

The 2019-21 state budget added $4.5 billion to school funding, from $22.8 billion to $27.3 billion, an increase of 20 percent in one budget cycle. Overall, spending on public education in Washington has doubled in eight years, rising from $13.5 billion in 2013 to $27.3 billion for the budget ending in 2021.

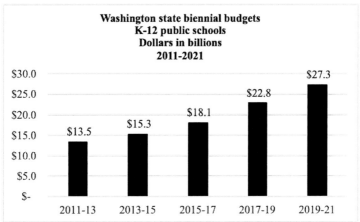

Spending on Washington public schools has doubled in eight years.

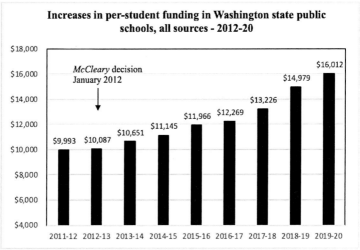

Per-student spending has increased sharply since the start of the *McCleary* case.

Public schools now receive more funding than private schools

Officials at Washington's public schools now receive $16,000 on average for the education of each student, a dramatic increase over the pre-McCleary level of $10,000 per student. Public school employees are now among the highest-paid workers in the state. By comparison, average private school tuition in Washington state is $9,680 for elementary schools and $12,560 for high schools.[1] Teachers' salaries and benefit levels at private schools are consistently lower than those of their peers in public schools.

The comparable numbers for Seattle are even higher. The 2019-20 budget for Seattle Public Schools is $1.04 billion, or $19,740 per student for 52,930 students.[2] Seattle Public Schools operates 101 public schools, to which children are assigned based on zip code.

Conclusion

Policymakers should publicly recognize that Washington schools now receive ample funding, should express gratitude to the hard-working taxpayers of the state and shift their focus to providing greater education choice to children and families.

2. Policy Recommendation: Increasing school spending has not improved student learning; structural reforms are needed

State officials have weakened the tests for measuring student learning many times.

Meanwhile, an objective federal standard, the National Assessment of Educational Progress (NAEP), referred to as the "Nation's Report Card," has been administered consistently to a statistically representative sample of Washington fourth and eighth-grade students in reading, math and science.

---

1 "Private School Review," Washington Private Schools, accessed May 10, 2019, at https://www.privateschoolreview.com/washington.
2 "Seattle Public Schools, 2019-2020 Recommended Budget," by Denise Juneau, Superintendent and School Board, at https://www.seattleschools.org/UserFiles/Servers/Server_543/File/District/Departments/Budget/2020%20Budget%20Development/recommended20.pdf.

The same test is administered to fourth and eighth-graders in other states. The NAEP is considered the most respected, reliable and consistent measure of academic progress in every state.

Test scores remain flat

In Washington, trends in academic learning by public school students, as measured by NAEP, have not improved over the past ten years. In spite of large spending increases, student learning levels remain largely flat.[3]

The poor results for children raise an important question: Why haven't the large increases in funding produced the improvements in student learning that its promoters promised?

One answer is that adding large increases in public funding to a bureaucratic and unwieldy education system prevents innovation, flexibility and professional creativity in the way students are taught. This finding is supported by experience, which shows that when the legislature increases funding for public schools, powerful political interests in the system focus first on policies that benefit themselves and then downgrade the goal of improving learning for children.

Public education is a monopoly

Since public education functions as a monopoly, there is little accountability and no career consequences for administrators or union executives due to failing test scores, a widening achievement gap and low graduation rates. As a result, the education system easily absorbs money to the benefit of established interests, while ineffective instructional programs continue unchanged.

---

3 "Trends in spending and learning in Washington's schools, 2006-2016," by Liv Finne, Legislative Memo, Washington Policy Center, January 2017, at http://www. washingtonpolicy.org/library/doclib/FINAL-PDF-Trends-in-Spending-and-LearningLiv-v2.pdf.

Examples of the rigid policy limits that prevent school districts from using money effectively include:

- Mis-allocated personnel – only about half of school district employees are classroom teachers;

- Low professional incentives – school administrators are barred by unions from offering bonuses or retention awards to the best teachers;

- Abuse and non-performance – union-imposed restrictions make it difficult to fire ineffective and abusive teachers;

- Restricting teacher recruitment – public schools may only hire applicants who have a special license, while private schools may hire any qualified applicant;

- Restricting teacher quality – schools of education hold monopoly power and are not held accountable for failing to train good teachers;

- Union financing – Unions make public school teachers pay dues, while union membership for private and public charter school teachers is completely voluntary;

- Ban on school choice – students are generally assigned to public schools on an involuntary basis based on zip code, while private school attendance is not restricted by geographical residence.

- Mis-allocated funding – Due to mandates, regulations and union requirements, only about 60 cents of every education dollar reaches the classroom in Washington.

Conclusion

For these reasons, lawmakers should enact structural reforms in public education that increase choice for parents and treat teachers like respected professionals, while recognizing that adding more money to an unreformed system won't help children.

3. Policy Recommendation: Expand access to charter schools

Charter schools are public schools that operate free from many of the restrictions placed on other public schools. With this local autonomy, teachers and principals in charter schools are able to create customized educational programs that better meet the learning needs of children, especially those living in underserved communities.

Another key difference between charter schools and traditional public schools is that children are not assigned to charter schools based on zip code. Parents voluntarily enroll their children in a charter school, while most public school children are assigned to a school by the central school district office, with little choice or input from parents.

Charter schools are popular with parents

The innovative and high-performing programs offered by public charter schools make them popular with parents. Charter schools are the most rapidly-expanding school choice innovation in public education since a public school teacher proposed the idea in the 1990s. Today, there are 7,000 charter schools across the country.[4]

Over the past ten years, charter school enrollment has increased from 1.3 million in 2007-08 to nearly 3.2 million students in 2017-18.[5]

---

4 "Charter School Datasets; Data Dashboard, 2019," National Alliance for Public Charter Schools, at https://data.publiccharters.org/.

5 "A Growing Movement; America's Largest Charter Public School Communities, Thirteenth Annual Edition," January 2019, by Kevin Hesla, Jamison White, and Adam Gerstenfeld, National Alliance for Public Charter Schools, at https://www.publiccharters.org/sites/default/files/documents/2019-03/rd1_napcs_enrollment_share_report%2003112019.pdf.

Research shows children attending charter schools are more likely to graduate from high school and to enroll in college.[6] Stanford University researchers found that learning gains in urban charter schools are dramatic. Urban charter schools add the equivalent of 28 days of additional learning in reading and 40 days of additional learning in math every year.

For low-income and minority students, the gains are 44 extra days of learning in reading and 59 extra days in math.[7] A recent Vanderbilt University study shows students attending charter high schools are more likely to stay in college and to experience higher earnings in the workforce.[8]

Washington voters approve charter schools

In 2012, Washington became the first state to legalize charter schools by passing a popular citizens' measure, Initiative 1240.[9] Unions immediately attacked the new law, gaining a ruling from the

Education

6 "Guide to Major Charter School Studies," by Liv Finne, Policy Brief, Washington Policy Center, July 23, 2012, at www.washingtonpolicy.org/ publications/detail/guide-to-major-charter-school-studies.

7 "A Rebuttal of Weingarten on the Facts," by Margaret Raymond, Director of the Center for Research on Education Outcomes (CREDO) at Stanford University, Huffpost Education, April 15, 2016, at www.huffingtonpost.com/ margaret-raymond/a-rebuttal-of-weingarten-_b_9701622.html.

8 "Charter High Schools' Effects on Long-Term Attainment and Earnings," by Tim R. Sass, Ron W. Zimmer, Brian P. Gill and T. Kevin Booker, Association for Public Policy Analysis and Management, Vanderbilt University, 2016, at news. vanderbilt.edu/files/pam_21913_Rev-FINAL-4416.pdf.

9 Initiative Measure No. 1240, "Concerns creation of a public charter school system," Office of the Secretary of State, General Election results, November 6, 2012, at results.vote.wa.gov/results/20121106/Initiative-Measure-No-1240-Concerns-creation-of-a-public-charter-school-system.html.

state supreme court that sought to shut down every charter school in the state.[10]

However, the legislature passed a bipartisan bill in 2016, which funds charter schools from the Opportunity Pathways Account.[11] Governor Jay Inslee, who opposes charter schools, reluctantly agreed to let the popular bill become law without his signature.

Washington has nine charter schools, located in Seattle, Kent, Spokane, Tukwila, Tacoma and Walla Walla. The schools are oversubscribed and maintain waiting lists of families seeking to enroll.

Sixty-three percent of the 3,500 students attending these schools come from low-income minority families. Many parents in Washington, particularly in underserved communities, regard charter schools as a better option for learning than their local public school.

Five new charter schools will soon open in Bellingham, Bremerton, Federal Way, South Seattle, Skyway, and Spokane.

State law limits the number of charter schools to 40, in a public system of more than 2,000 schools. Forty charter schools are clearly insufficient to meet the current needs of families, let alone the increasing needs of underserved families in the future.

---

10 *League of Women Voters of Washington, El Centro de la Raza, Washington Association of School Administrators, Washington Education Association, Wayne Au, Pat Braman, Donna Boyer, and Sarah Lucas v. State of Washington*, en banc opinion, Supreme Court of the State of Washington, September 4, 2015, No. 89714-0, at www.courts.wa.gov/opinions/pdf/897140.pdf.
11 ESSSB 6194, "Concerning public schools that are not common schools," enacted April 3, 2016, without Governor Inslee's signature, at app.leg.wa.gov/billinfo/summary.aspx?bill=6194&year=2015.

Repeal the cap on charter schools

Lawmakers should repeal the artificial limit on the number of public charter schools that can serve children in the state. Given their popularity with parents, and the bipartisan support of the charter school law, lifting the limit is well within the ability of the legislature. Expanding family access to charter schools is part of fulfilling the state's paramount constitutional duty to make ample provision for the education of all children living within the state.[12]

Provide charter schools local levy and capital funding

Charter schools receive state and federal funding, but they are denied local levy funding. Local levy funding amounts to about $2,300 per student on average, about 17 percent of operating revenue for most public schools.

In Seattle, local taxpayers supplement the public schools with $3,000 in local levy funds per student, money charter schools do not get. Charter school families in Seattle must pay local school taxes like everyone else, but their children are not allowed to benefit from the resulting levy revenue.

Officials have also cut funding for classrooms, buildings and other facilities so that charter public schools actually have to pay rent.

Fairness and equity require giving Washington charter schools the same local levy and capital funding other public schools receive. No one wants a system that gives minority children less money for their education than other children receive.

Education

---

12 "Article IX, Section 1, Education," Constitution of the State of Washington, at leg.wa.gov/LawsAndAgencyRules/Pages/constitution.aspx.

---

4. Policy Recommendation: Expand access to family choice in education

Over the past 20 years, officials in most states have recognized that parents need greater family choice in public education because it improves learning outcomes for children.

Helping parents get involved in making education decisions is the purpose of school choice programs. These programs provide a variety of ways, including scholarships, vouchers, tax-credit programs, Education Savings Accounts, charter schools and online learning, that give parents the means to decide how their children are educated.

Family choice in education is common in other states

Family choice programs are now common across the country. Thirty states and the District of Columbia operate 65 family choice learning programs that fund the education of more than 480,000 students.[13] Under these programs, families direct the public education funding to which they are entitled to the private school of their choice.

Family choice programs include directing funding to public schools as well. The key is that parents, not central office bureaucrats, direct resources in the best interest of children. Parent choice in education improves public schools by giving administrators a strong incentive to serve families first, ahead of entrenched political interests in the system.

The education monopoly provides less service at higher costs

Without incentives, school districts often provide less service at

---

13 "The ABC's of School Choice, 2019 Edition," by Robert C. Enlow, *Ed Choice*, at https://www.edchoice.org/research/the-abcs-of-school-choice/.

higher costs, and suffer recurring union strikes, because the career professionals know the education monopoly will protect them, even when schools fail to educate students.

Efforts to hold schools accountable have not worked. Accountability measures are routinely manipulated to create the appearance of improvement when, in reality, the rigor of academic learning standards is being reduced.

For example, in August 2015, the Washington State Board of Education lowered the standard for passing state tests in English and math from a 3 to a 2.5, breaking its promise to make all students "college and career ready."[14] Another example is how the state Superintendent of Public Instruction permits districts artificially to inflate graduation statistics by excluding those students most likely to drop out; that is, students enrolled in a drop-out re-engagement program.[15]

Family choice creates accountability

Family choice in education creates real accountability. Parents care about the needs of their children, and cannot be gamed, threatened or silenced. School choice allows parents assigned to low-performing schools the option of sending their children to an alternative school or online program that meets their needs and, most importantly, to direct their children's public education funding to where it will do the most good.

At the same time, choice programs create powerful incentives for traditional systems to improve. School choice gives central

14 "State Board of Education sets lower bar on Common Core tests," by Donna Blankenship, Associated Press, August 5, 2015, at komonews.com/news/local/state-board-of-education-sets-lower-bar-on-common-core-tests.

15 "State policy artificially boosts district-level grad rates by leaving out some at-risk students," by Ashley Gross, KNKX Radio, April 23, 2019, at https://www.knkx.org/post/state-policy-artificially-boosts-district-level-grad-rates-leaving-out-some-risk-students.

district administrators a reason to reform their schools, so they do not lose families to the available alternatives. An academic review of 33 empirical education studies found that 32 of them concluded school choice policies have a beneficial effect on traditional schools.[16]

The highest-quality research shows students gain from having school choice, and that traditional school systems respond to school choice by improving their services for children.[17]

School choice is popular with all groups

Seventy-three percent of voters surveyed in a June 2019 nationwide poll said they support school choice programs that give "parents the right to use tax dollars designated for their child's education to send their child to the public or private school which best serves their needs."[18]

Conclusion

The pro-school choice coalition is bipartisan and diverse, with majority support from Latinos (73 percent) African Americans (67 percent), and Millennials (75 percent).[19] Support for private school

---

16 "A Win-Win Solution; The Empirical Evidence on School Choice," by Greg Forster, *Ed Choice*, May 2016, at https://www.edchoice.org/wp-content/uploads/2016/05/2016-5- Win-Win-Solution-WEB.pdf.

17 "Choosing to Learn," by Joseph Bast, Jason Bedrick, Lindsey Burke, Andrew J. Coulson, Robert C. Enlow, Kara Kerwin, and Herbert J. Walberg, CATO Institute Commentary, March 12, 2014, at https://www.cato.org/publications/commentary/choosing-learn.

18 "2019 National School Choice Poll," American Federation for Children, June 2019, at https://www.federationforchildren.org/2019-national-school-choice-poll/. See also "Joseph Lieberman: School Choice is a winning policy, so why don't Democrats support it?" by Senator Joseph Lieberman, Fox News Channel, July 22, 2019, at https://www.foxnews.com/opinion/joe-lieberman-school-choice-democrats-2020-election.

19 Ibid.

---

scholarships grows to 83 percent for families with special needs children.[20]

5. Policy Recommendation: Allow special needs children access to state-funded Education Savings Accounts

Lawmakers should provide $15,000 a year in direct aid to families with special needs children to pay for private education services. Parents would receive a deposit of public funds into a government-issued Education Savings Account (ESA) with restricted, learning-focused uses.

Families and caseworkers could use the money to pay for specialized services from private tutors and private schools for the children. The state treasurer would audit ESAs to ensure the money is used for education. Participating students would take a nationally-recognized test in math and English to demonstrate progress in learning.

ESAs in other states

The states of Arizona, Florida, Mississippi, Tennessee and North Carolina already provide an ESA to their special needs families. Twelve states give special needs families direct assistance to attend private schools, and South Carolina provides both a tax credit scholarship and a direct tax credit to help special needs families.

By contrast, Washington's special education system is highly centralized, wasteful and bureaucratic.

---

20 "2017 National School Choice Poll," American Federation for Children, January 2017, at https://www.federationforchildren.org/poll-public-support-school-choice-remains-strong-supportive-federal-movement-increase-school-choice/.

Parents often complain about district reluctance to evaluate a child for an Individual Education Plan (IEP), and about the mediocre quality of evaluations that are conducted. If a child is granted an IEP, parents say it often contains vague goals and objectives, and that their children don't receive an appropriate public education.

Administrators of the public schools always say the solution is more money. But adding more money won't help children stymied by outdated teaching methods, insensitive bureaucracies and restrictive union rules. More money will not solve the problem of imposing a standardized system on the unique learning needs of these vulnerable children.

Conclusion

Lawmakers should provide fully-funded Education Savings Accounts so that families with special needs receive the best services immediately. This would not only benefit children, but it would also show that lawmakers care more about helping special needs children than about funding a bureaucratic legacy system.

6. Policy Recommendation: Provide a $15,000 tax credit to fund a private school option for foster children

Children are placed in the care of the state because a judge has decided a particular home setting is dangerous and that separating the child from parents is in the child's best interest. Such homes are characterized by parents involved in crime, drug or alcohol abuse, low rates of marriage, disruptive or chaotic daily routine and abuse of children through direct harm or neglect.[21]

---

21 "Guide to Supporting Students in Foster Care," by Washington State Department of Health and Human Services, Office of Superintendent of Public Instruction and Treehouse, 2018, page 12, at https://www. treehouseforkids.org/ wp-content/uploads/2018/01/ treehouse2017final2ndedinteractive.pdf.

In 2017, Washington had 10,068 children in foster care. Some 2,167 of these children have no home to return to and are awaiting adoption into a stable, permanent family.[22] About 4,500 of Washington foster children are of school age, and, as required by state law, they have been placed by caseworkers in local public schools.[23]

Children in foster care often fail in public schools

Foster children face many problems in obtaining an education from the current system of public education. Common systematic failures experienced by foster children include:

- Changing schools during the school year;
- Late enrollment after a change of residence;
- Lost, missing, or incomplete school records;
- Assigned to a low-performing school;
- Lack of stable adult advisors;
- Learning delays in reading, math, and writing;
- Increased social and emotional stress;
- High drop-out rate.[24]

As a result, less than half of students in foster care in Washington state graduate from high school on time, resulting

22 "Washington foster care and adoption guidelines," AdoptUSKids, accessed October 16, 2018, at https:// www.adoptuskids.org/adoption-and-foster-care/ how-toadopt-and-foster/state-information/washington.
23 Ibid.
24 "Barriers to Improving Educational Outcomes for Foster Youth," Foster Children and Youth Educational Technical Assistance Mental Health Advocacy Services, Inc., 2003, funded by the Stuart Foundation, at http:// users.neo. registeredsite.com/3/8/9/12669983/assets/ Barriers-FYEd2003.pdf.

in increased social disruption and reduced chances for success in life.[25]

Barriers created by state law

Currently, state lawmakers generally bar foster children and foster youth from accessing educational services provided by private schools, even in cases when state case managers know such services would be in the best interests of the child.

Creating a school choice scholarship program for foster children

HB 1969, a bill introduced in 2019 by Representative Chris Corry (R-Yakima), would improve access to quality educational services for foster children by creating a school choice scholarship program.[26] HB 1969 would generate private funds through a tax credit to provide children and youth in foster care the option of attending a public or private school that is in the best interest of the child.

Foster child scholarships would be funded by providing a Business and Occupation tax credit of equal value to those who make a voluntary contribution to the program. Scholarships would provide the lesser of $15,000 or the annual cost of attending an approved, participating school.[27]

---

25 "Educational Outcomes for Foster Youth – Benchmarks," Washington State Institute for Public Policy, December 2012, at http://www.wsipp.wa.gov/ ReportFile/1115/ Wsipp_Educational-Outcomes-of-Foster-YouthBenchmarks_ Full-Report.pdf.

26 HB 1969, an Act relating to creating and funding a school choice scholarship program for foster students, Section 1, Subsection 2(d)(ii), at: http://lawfilesext. leg.wa.gov/biennium/2019-20/Pdf/Bills/House%20 Bills/1969.pdf. Co-sponsors of HB 1969 are Representatives Dan Griffey, Michelle Caldier, Brandon Vick, Larry Hoff, Bob McCaslin and Andrew Barkis. The bill was introduced February 8, 2019.

27 Ibid.

The value of an individual tax credit would be limited to $200,000, and the total value of the program would be limited to $20 million a year.[28]

Conclusion

Eighteen states now provide 22 different tax credit scholarship programs. These programs allow children who are low-income, special needs and assigned to low-performing schools the opportunity to attend a private school.[29] Lawmakers should create a similar program for Washington's foster children.

7. Policy Recommendation: Avoid failed reforms that have not improved schools

For the past decade, the state of Washington has pursued the policy of increasing funding to the schools. Included in the reforms pushed by the 2012 *McCleary* decision of the state supreme court is the Prototypical School Model. This model mandates restrictive staffing ratios and creating twenty work categories, like "media specialist," "social worker" and "technology staff." This funding model also required Washington state to pay for smaller class sizes.

This funding model serves the interests of the union because it requires the hiring of a certain number of staff, but it has provided little lasting benefit for students. Student learning has remained flat, even as district payrolls have swelled with increased staff, specialists and paid union executives.

---

28 Ibid.
29 The eighteen states are Alabama, Arizona, Florida, Georgia, Illinois, Indiana, Iowa, Kansas, Louisiana, Montana, Nevada, New Hampshire, Oklahoma, Pennsylvania, Rhode Island, South Carolina, South Dakota, and Virginia.

WEA union diverted class size reduction money to higher pay for staff

Lawmakers approved more than $500 million in the 2017-19 state budget for reduced class sizes.[30] They promised class sizes of 17 students in grades K-3, 27 students in grades 4-6, and 28 students in grades 7-12.[31]

Then, in the fall of 2018, the WEA union lobbyists targeted class size reduction funding to be transferred to provide additional, double-digit pay increases to staff.

This pattern is repeated over and over again. The WEA union loudly promotes a popular program that is supposed to help students to demand more money for schools. A few months after more money is approved, WEA executives threaten illegal strikes to close schools if the money is not diverted to provide pay raises. Out of fear of continued controversy and bullying, school administrators usually give in, and children are deprived of promised services.

The failure of high-stakes testing

In 1993 policymakers passed legislation to require students to take the Washington Assessment of Student Learning (WASL) in the belief that high-stakes testing would create incentives for the schools to improve. Testing was supposed to be the state's public education accountability measure.

---

30 "Is Seattle Public Schools bargaining away class size reduction money?" by Liv Finne, Washington Policy Center, August 16, 2018, at https://www. washingtonpolicy.org/publications/detail/is-seattle-public-schools-bargaining-away-class-size-reduction-money.
31 "Operating Budget, 2019-21," Engrossed Substitute House Bill 1109, passed April 28, 2019 and signed by Governor Inslee on May 21, 2019, at https://app. leg.wa.gov/billsummary?BillNumber=1109&Year=2019&Initiative=false.

Twenty years later, Governor Gregoire repealed the WASL requirement. Then in 2014, Governor Inslee adopted the weaker Smarter Balanced Assessment Consortium test, and in 2019 he ended all requirements that students pass a high-stakes test to earn a high school diploma.

Routine testing is an important tool for educators to assess where students stand and to identify areas where they need extra help. Mandated high-stakes testing, however, failed to create accountability for teachers and administrators in the system. The WEA union vigorously resisted public accountability and urged parents to boycott the tests.

Conclusion

The political experience in Olympia shows that top-down, mandated high-stakes testing does not work and that real accountability is only achieved when parents have access to broad school choice so that children can be moved to where they receive the best-quality learning.

8. Policy Recommendation: Repeal lifetime tenure and certification rules that keep the best teachers out of public schools

Washington state law bars anyone from teaching in a public school who does not have an approved certificate. This ban does not apply, however, to private schools. This is one reason private schools are consistently better than public ones. A Harvard Graduate School of Education study found that a formal teaching certificate "matters little" in raising student classroom achievement.[32]

---

32 "Photo Finish: Teacher certification doesn't guarantee a winner," by Thomas J. Kane, Jonah E. Rockoff and Douglas O. Staiger, *Education Next*, 2008, at educationnext.org/photo-finish/.

Teaching certificates do not assure teacher quality

Harvard researchers found that a teacher's mastery of subject matter is far more important to student learning than a state-issued certificate. In theory, an official certificate is supposed to assure teacher quality. In the real world of classrooms and children, however, there is a marked difference between paper certificate requirements and being a good teacher.

The legislature has granted private schools the advantage of hiring based on quality and experience rather than paper credentials. Many private schools hire quality faculty who hold doctorate degrees or are experienced business professionals but do not hold formal teaching certificates.

These are not elite private schools; they are often located in low-income neighborhoods and their teachers take on the noble work of educating the hardest-to-teach students. Lawmakers should allow public schools to recruit the best classroom talent available on an equal basis as their private-sector counterparts.

Effective teachers raise student achievement

Teacher tenure laws grant automatic lifetime employment to public school teachers after three years, making it nearly impossible to fire a bad teacher in a public school. Private schools, in contrast, may hire and fire teachers at will, allowing private schools to dismiss poor performers and continuously improve teacher quality.

Research shows that an effective teacher in the classroom is more important than any other factor, including smaller class size, in raising student achievement.[33] A good teacher can make as much as a full year's difference in the learning growth of students.[34]

Students taught by a high-quality teacher three years in a row score 50 percentile points higher on standardized tests than students of weak teachers.[35] The research also shows that students taught by a weak teacher two years in a row may never catch up.

The research indicates the best teachers have the following qualities:[36]

- Mastery of the subject matter;

- Five years or more of teaching experience;

- Training in content knowledge and high levels of classroom competency;

- Strong academic skills, curiosity and excitement about learning for its own sake.

Improving teacher quality is far more cost-effective than reducing class size

Research shows that, compared to having an effective teacher, smaller class size benefits are minor. A strong teacher can deliver a year more of learning to students than a weak teacher. Lawmakers

33 "Teacher Pay, The Political Implications of Recent Research," by Dan Goldhaber, University of Washington and Urban Institute, The Center for American Progress, December 2006, at www.americanprogress.org/issues/2006/12/teacher_pay.html.
34 Ibid.
35 "Cumulative and Residual Effects of Teachers on Future Student Academic Achievement," by William L. Sanders and June C. Rivers, Value-Added Research and Assessment Center, University of Tennessee, November 1996, at www.mccsc.edu/~curriculum/cumulative%20and%20 residual%20effects%20 of%20teachers.pdf.
36 "Teacher quality and student achievement research review," by Policy Studies Associates for the Center for Public Education, November 2005, at www.centerforpubliceducation.org/site/ c.kjJXJ5MPIwE/b.1510983/.

should enact policies that improve teacher quality, which is a far more cost-effective strategy than reducing class sizes and is much better for students.[37]

Creating renewed respect for teachers

Teachers should be hired based on knowledge and a sense of excitement about the subject they will present to students. Teachers who show results, regardless of certification status, should be rewarded and encouraged. Teachers who do not should be dismissed, regardless of artificial certification and tenure rules.

Conclusion

Lawmakers can level the playing field by repealing lifetime tenure rules and ending the limits on teacher hiring to allow public schools to hire the best teachers while drawing new talent into the profession. The result would be renewed respect for teachers and, most importantly, a better learning environment for public school students.

---

37 "Students First – Why an effective teachers matters: A Q & A with Eric Hanushek," by Eric Hanushek, Stanford University, Hoover Institution, February 2011, at http://hanushek.stanford.edu/opinions/students-first-why-effective-teacher-matters-q-eric-hanushek.

Additional resources

"Update on charter schools: Legislature continues funding discrimination against charter school families," by Liv Finne, Policy Brief, Washington Policy Center, September 2019

"School Funding in the 2019 Legislative Session: Washington state public schools now receive more money than most private schools," by Liv Finne, Policy Notes, Washington Policy Center, July 2019

"HB 1969, to create and fund a tax credit scholarship for foster care children," by Liv Finne, Legislative Memo, Washington Policy Center, March 2019

"A relic of anti-religious bigotry, Washington's Blaine Amendment should no longer block school choice for families," by Liv Finne, Legislative Memo, Washington Policy Center, February 2019

"Public funding of private schools in Washington state," by Liv Finne, Policy Brief, Washington Policy Center, November 2018

"New government report shows massive $9.7 billion increase in education spending provided no improvement for Washington students," by Liv Finne, Policy Notes, Washington Policy Center, April 2018

"Overview of public school choice programs: How national and state-level public school choice improves learning opportunities for families and children," by Liv Finne, Policy Brief, Washington Policy Center, October 2017

"Education Money for Families: How Education Savings Accounts can help children learn in Washington state," by Liv Finne, Policy Brief, Washington Policy Center, January 2016

CHAPTER SIX
OPEN AND ACCOUNTABLE GOVERNMENT

1. Policy Recommendation: Provide remote testimony services for citizens

The legislature has made significant progress in implementing Washington Policy Center's recommendation to provide remote testimony for Washingtonians. First, the Senate decided to make its trial use of remote testimony services permanent, while the House, in 2019, finally took steps toward embracing this commonsense transparency reform by authorizing a study.

Remote testimony services allow ordinary people from around the state to participate in a public hearing through a video hook-up, without the time and expense of traveling to Olympia. Remote testimony is popular with citizens and with lawmakers as well. Discussing the importance of providing remote testimony services, Senate Majority Leader Andy Billig said:

> "Technology offers us an opportunity to open up the doors of government to more people across the state. Everyone should feel like they can have their voice heard in Olympia, regardless of where you live. Our democracy is stronger when more people are involved, and this offers another method to weigh in on pertinent issues without driving to Olympia."[1]

Making remote testimony available at all legislative hearings

Due to its success, Washington's current remote testimony

---

1 "Remote testimony is here to stay in Senate," by Jason Mercier, Washington Policy Center, January 30, 2019, at https://www.washingtonpolicy.org/publications/detail/remote-testimony-is-here-to-stay-in-senate.

program should be extended to include House committee hearings and all Senate hearings. Allowing the public to give remote testimony from fixed locations around the state would give citizens greater opportunity to be part of the lawmaking process.

It would also help Washingtonians avoid difficult travel during the winter months when the legislature is in session, especially when the snowy Cascade Mountains sometimes cut Eastern Washington off from the state capitol.

Avoiding travel to Olympia

Even in mild seasons, getting to Olympia to attend a public hearing requires a full day of travel for many Washingtonians. Consider the following driving distances under even the best traffic conditions:

- Spokane to Olympia............320 miles
- Walla Walla to Olympia......305 miles
- Kennewick to Olympia........258 miles
- Bellingham to Olympia ......149 miles
- Vancouver to Olympia........106 miles
- Everett to Olympia...............89 miles

Remote testimony can instantly overcome these distances and provide all Washingtonians the chance to be part of the legislative process. According to the National Conference of State Legislatures, several states already provide a remote testimony service for their citizens.

Conclusion

Although there is broad support for allowing remote testimony, there is concern that it would be disruptive to the current hearing process. To avoid disruptions, committees should establish preset rules for those wishing to provide remote testimony. The Washington state Senate provides the public with an online resource that describes this process.[2]

2. Policy Recommendation: Improve public notice and ban the use of title-only bills

Washington's lawmakers have adopted rules on paper that let the public participate in the legislative debate, but the casual way they routinely waive the rules undercuts these important public protections.

The state House of Representatives says one of its official goals is to "increase public participation, understanding, and transparency of the legislative process ..." and to "enact high-quality legislation through debate and collaboration that is thoughtful and responsive, and honors our diverse citizenry."[3]

This commonsense principle reflects a fundamental premise of our democracy: Citizens should be able to comment on the proposed laws we have to live under to ensure lawmakers are informed about the public's opinions and expectations.

Notice for public hearings

The legislature's rules require that:

"At least five days' notice shall be given of all public hearings held by any committee other than the rules committee. Such notice shall contain the date, time and place of such

2 "Senate Remote Testimony Overview," Washington state Senate, accessed September 6, 2019, at http://leg.wa.gov/Senate/Committees/Pages/RemoteTestimony.aspx.
3 "House Mission Resolution," Washington State Legislature, passed January 18, 2006, at http://leg.wa.gov/House/Documents/HouseResolution.pdf.

hearing together with the title and number of each bill, or identification of the subject matter, to be considered at such hearing."[4]

The rules also supposedly prohibit so-called title-only bills, a blank bill with a title and a number, but empty pages where text will be filled in later.

Lawmakers have a practice, however, of introducing title-only bills that have all the attributes of formal legislation – an assigned bill number, sponsor names, date of introduction, referral to committee – but no text.

Title-only bills are not a transparent way to introduce changes to state law. They are essentially used by lawmakers to circumvent the state constitution. New bills are not supposed to be considered in the last ten days of the legislative session, unless two-thirds of lawmakers agree, as provided under Article 2, Section 36 of the state constitution.

Title-only bills as placeholders

To get around this constitutional restriction, some lawmakers introduce title-only bills late in the session as a placeholder, so they can put in the real text later without having to secure the required two-thirds vote.

If lawmakers feel the state constitution is getting in the way of being transparent and providing adequate public notice, it would be better for them to propose repeal of Article 2, Section 36 and replace it with meaningful legislative transparency protections that would:

---

4 "Permanent Rules of the Senate," Washington State Legislature, accessed April 11, 2016, at http://leg.wa.gov/Senate/Administration/Pages/senate_rules. aspx.

- Provide mandatory public notice and waiting periods before legislative action;

- Ban title-only bills, and;

- Subject the Legislature to the same transparency requirements that are placed on local governments.

Adopting these transparency protections and ending the practice of title-only bills would help lawmakers fulfill their promised goal, stated in their formal House Resolution, to "increase public participation, understanding, and transparency of the legislative process."

Efforts to increase legislative transparency

In 2013, lawmakers introduced proposals to implement these legislative transparency requirements (Senate Bill 6560 and its companion House Bill 2369), but these measures did not receive a public hearing.

The most blatant abuse of this process occurred during the 2019 legislative session when lawmakers used the device to impose a massive last-minute tax increase on financial institutions. The measure imposed new costs across the economy and, because it targeted out-of-state banks, was of questionable constitutionality. The public had almost no chance to comment on the bill before it became law.

The lack of public process on that tax increase (HB 2167) was so poor that those subject to the tax were provided only a few hours' notice of the details before the hastily called public hearing. Testifying on the bill, Trent House with the Washington Banking Association said:

"We found out about it (tax bill) about three-and-a-half hours ago. That's very difficult to process even with the best staff, it's hard to get information back on a bill of this nature that raises this kind of money in that period of time… We haven't seen a fiscal note. We don't know exactly what this bill does or who it applies to. It's very difficult to even understand how to testify on this bill not knowing that information."[5]

Boosting public confidence in how laws are made

SB 6560, introduced in 2013, would have improved notice of public hearings and banned title-only bills. It would have forced the legislature to make public decisions the same open way that city and county officials across the state do. It would have prevented committees from going into recess, as members negotiate secret agreements on amendments, then coming back into public session to vote on them formally.

Conclusion

Lawmakers should enact legislation like SB 6560 to enhance transparency and bolster public confidence in the lawmaking process.

3. Policy recommendation: Apply the Public Records Act and the Open Public Meetings Act to the legislature

All state and local government agencies in Washington are subject to the Public Records Act and the Open Public Meetings Act. The legislature, however, claims it is exempt from full disclosure. The exemption has been challenged in court, but regardless of the outcome, the legislature should follow the same

---

5 HB 2167, relating to tax revenue," House Finance Committee, Washington Legislature, April 26, 2019, TVW.org, and quoted in "Governor asked to veto stealth tax increase due to transparency concerns," by Jason Mercier, Washington Policy Center, at https://www.washingtonpolicy.org/publications/detail/governor-asked-to-veto-stealth-tax-increase-due-to-transparency-concerns.

disclosure and transparency requirements that the law places on county and local government officials.

Full disclosure of public records

Nearly all local government records and internal communications are subject to public disclosure, but members of the legislature and their staff claim special treatment and do not routinely release emails and other internal policy related records to the public.

This double standard understandably irritates local government officials, who must operate under a different standard of disclosure. It is also a disservice to citizens, who are denied the fullest disclosure of the records and activities of their state lawmakers.

Conclusion

As the most powerful representative body in the state, the legislature should lead by example and subject itself to all the requirements of the Public Record Act and Open Public Meetings Act, on the same basis as other public entities in Washington.

4. Policy Recommendation: Require a two-thirds vote of the legislature to change a voter-approved initiative

Article 1, Section 1 of the state constitution says:

"All political power is inherent in the people, and governments derive their just powers from the consent of the governed, and are established to protect and maintain individual rights."

The clear authority of the people over their government means that, before any legislative powers are granted, the people reserve for themselves co-equal lawmaking authority. This sovereign authority is explained in Article 2, Section 1:

"The legislative authority... shall be vested in the legislature, but the people reserve to themselves the power to propose bills, laws, and to enact or reject the same at the polls, independent of the legislature, and also reserve power, at their own option, to approve or reject at the polls any act, item, section, or part of any bill, act, or law passed by the legislature. (a) Initiative: The first power reserved by the people is the initiative."

Despite reserving this power to enact laws, it is very difficult for citizens to qualify an initiative for consideration. The number of valid signatures needed to put an initiative on the ballot is eight percent of the votes cast for Governor in the most recent general election, or 259,622 valid signatures.[6]

Protecting voter-passed laws

To ensure these laws enacted by the people are not immediately discarded by the legislature, Article 2, Section 41 of the constitution requires a two-thirds vote of lawmakers to amend a voter-approved initiative within the first two years of passage. After two years, only a simple majority vote in the legislature is required to amend or repeal a popular initiative.

The two-year protection for voter-passed initiatives may have been sufficient at one time, but the legislature's frequent practice of amending initiatives and attaching an emergency clause to the

---

6 "Frequently Asked Questions about Circulating Initiative and Referendum Petitions," Elections and Voting, Office of the Secretary of State, Olympia, Washington, accessed September 19, 2019, at https://www.sos.wa.gov/elections/initiatives/faq.aspx.

changes is denying the people an opportunity to stop the legislature from quickly gutting voter-passed laws.

Respecting basic constitutional powers

Article 2, Section 1 should be amended to remove the two-year expiration of the two-thirds vote requirement, and to require permanently a two-thirds vote for lawmakers to change laws enacted by the people.

Conclusion

If the legislature cannot secure a two-thirds vote to amend an initiative, lawmakers by a simple majority should propose a ballot referendum seeking voter ratification of the proposed changes. This would allow the voters a final say on the legislature's desired changes and would respect the people's basic constitutional power as co-equal lawmakers.

5. Policy Recommendation: Reduce the number of statewide elected offices

At present, the people of Washington elect officials to nine statewide offices (not counting justices to the state supreme court). These offices are Governor, Lieutenant Governor, Secretary of State, Treasurer, Auditor, Attorney General, Superintendent of Public Instruction, Commissioner of Public Lands and Insurance Commissioner. Yet for many years there has been a debate about whether this is the most effective way to structure our state government.

One view holds that the best approach is using the "long ballot" to institute the greatest amount of direct democracy, by requiring election of a large number of high-level state officials. This reasoning dates from views held during the Progressive Era of the early 1900s.

Short ballot promotes public accountability

Others argue a "short ballot" approach is better because the people choose a limited number of top officials, who are then held uniquely responsible for the proper functioning of government. Proponents of this view say that, in practice, most people don't know who is elected to minor statewide offices and that elected officials are subject to greater public scrutiny when there are fewer of them.

All statewide elected offices, except for Insurance Commissioner, are established by the state constitution. The Insurance Commissioner is also the only one for which the legislature, not the constitution, has established the elective nature of the office.

Duties of many elected offices are just like appointed positions

In contrast to the nine elected positions, all other senior officials in the executive branch are appointed by the Governor. They make up the Governor's cabinet and include many important positions. Here are some examples:

- Secretary of Social and Health Services;
- Director of Ecology;
- Director of Labor and Industries;
- Director of Agriculture;
- Director of Financial Management;
- Secretary of Transportation;
- Director of Licensing;

- Director of General Administration;

- Director of Revenue;

- Director of Retirement Systems;

- Secretary of Corrections;

- Chief of the State Patrol.

The duties and responsibilities of these appointed officials are similar to, and often more important than, those of minor elected officials, like the Secretary of State, Superintendent of Public Instruction, Commissioner of Public Lands or Insurance Commissioner.

Ending policy conflicts within the executive branch

Today, Washington's eight other statewide elected officials are independent of the Governor. They lobby the legislature independently and even work against what the Governor is trying to accomplish. Any such conflict is easily resolved in departments that are administered by appointees. If a policy disagreement arises among cabinet officers, the Governor settles it by formulating a single, unified policy for his administration, or by dismissing the offending cabinet officer.

Similarly, if the legislature is unable to reach an agreement with a cabinet official over important legislation, the dispute can be taken "over his head" to the Governor. The Governor may or may not agree with the position the cabinet appointee has taken, but at least the legislature will get a final answer. The legislature would know that, through the Governor, the executive branch speaks with one voice.

Increasing the accountability of the Governor

The reason this works is that the Governor has direct authority over the performance of appointed officials. They serve at his pleasure and are answerable to him. The Governor, in turn, must report to the voters for the overall performance of the administration.

Conclusion

The state constitution should be amended to abolish the Secretary of State, Superintendent of Public Instruction and Commissioner of Public Lands as independently-elected statewide officials. The way the Insurance Commissioner is selected can be changed by the legislature.

These four positions should then be restructured as cabinet agencies headed by appointees, making the Governor fully accountable to the people for the actions of these departments of the executive branch.

6. Policy Recommendation: Amend the constitution to allow district elections for supreme court justices

Under the constitution, all state supreme court justices are elected statewide. This increases the costs of these races and in practice means that most candidates come from the Puget Sound region. As currently conducted, supreme court elections do not provide geographic and cultural representation on the state's highest court.

To improve geographic representation on the supreme court, elections should be changed to district elections. This would provide more regional diversity and help reduce the cost of running for office while providing candidates more time to focus on voter outreach, debates and forums in their area of the state.

Only one of the nine justices on the court once lived in Eastern Washington at the time of taking office appointment. Had Justice

Debra Stephens not won election, *all* of the state's supreme court justices would be from the Puget Sound region.

In recent years, any justices who did come from Eastern Washington got their start on the court through appointment. Justice Stephens was appointed by Governor Gregoire. Justice Richard P. Guy was appointed by Governor Gardner. Recent practice shows that unless a Governor makes an appointment, Eastern Washington is unlikely to be represented on the state supreme court.

Improving geographical representation on the court

Justices are not elected as representatives, but they are charged with making impartial decisions, and the life experiences of those who serve on the court are important in making those decisions. Many people argue that gender and ethnicity diversity should be represented on the court. The same could be said of geographic and cultural diversity across Washington state.

Election by district is a well-established system for choosing justices. Ten states use districts for the election or appointment of justices:

- Four states, Illinois, Louisiana, Kentucky and Mississippi, elect justices by district;

- Six states, Florida, Maryland, Nebraska, Oklahoma, South Dakota and Tennessee, appoint justices by district.

Conclusion

Changing to district elections for supreme court justices would make the highest court fully reflective of "One Washington," rather than a part of a state government dominated by the Puget Sound region. District elections would create more choices for voters, reduce election costs, and encourage more qualified people to run for public office.

7. Policy Recommendation: Require that mail-in ballots be received by election day

Because Washington requires ballots only to be postmarked, not delivered, by election day, it is difficult to declare winners on election night.

Instead of an election day, we have an election month. A month of campaigning, followed by a month of waiting. The problem with holding a month-long election is the public cynicism and distrust it unnecessarily breeds in the state's election results, as vote-leading candidates shift position days and weeks after the election.

A better system

Other states use a better system. Oregon has all-mail voting too, but, unlike Washington, state ballots must be received by 8:00 p.m. on election day to be counted.

According to Oregon election official Brenda Bayes, this process is working just as voters intended when they adopted this requirement in 1998. Bayes notes:

> "Our office typically does not receive complaints regarding a voter feeling like they are disenfranchised solely based upon the 8:00 p.m. restriction... Oregon voters appear to appreciate that they are able to have unofficial results quickly after the 8:00 p.m. deadline regarding candidates and measures. If Oregon were to go to a postmark deadline it would delay these unofficial results."

Former Washington Secretary of State Sam Reed was a strong supporter of requiring that mail-in ballots arrive by election day. Reed said:

> "I have long supported a requirement that ballots be returned to the county elections offices, by mail or dropbox, by election day. Neighboring Oregon, which pioneered vote-by-mail via a citizen initiative more than a decade ago, has found that good voter education and steady reminders of the return deadline have produced excellent results."[7]

As noted by the National Council of State Legislatures,

> "All-mail elections may slow down the vote counting process, especially if a state's policy is to allow ballots postmarked by election day to be received and counted in the days and weeks after the election."[8]

According to the National Association of Secretaries of State, the vast majority of states require mail-in ballots to actually be received by election day. In fact, the other all vote-by-mail states (Oregon and Colorado) require ballots to be received by election day.

Conclusion

To avoid concerns about possible voter disenfranchisement, military ballots could be exempted from the election day deadline, along with any ballots postmarked the Friday before the election. Those wishing to send in their ballots after that date could use a

---

7 "Polls point to weeks of waiting for election results," by Jason Mercier, Washington Policy Center, October 24, 2012, at https://www.washingtonpolicy.org/publications/detail/polls-point-to-weeks-of-waiting-for-election-results.

8 "All-Mail Elections (aka Vote-By-Mail)," by Dylan Lynch, National Council of State Legislatures (NCSL), June 27, 2019, at http://www.ncsl.org/research/elections-and-campaigns/all-mail-elections.aspx.

secure ballot dropbox before the election period ended. This is exactly what occurs for Oregon, Colorado and those counties in California that use all vote-by-mail.

Additional resources

"It is impossible to analyze a title-only bill, because the text is blank," by Jason Mercier, Legislative Memo, Washington Policy Center, April 2019

"House proposes remote testimony resolution," by Jason Mercier, Washington Policy Center, March 11, 2019

"Timeline: Legislative public records debate," by Jason Mercier, Washington Policy Center, February 23, 2018

"District elections for supreme court gets public hearing," by Jason Mercier, Washington Policy Center, January 29, 2015

"And the election winner is...to be determined," by Jason Mercier, Washington Policy Center, November 3, 2014

"Time to add to the nearly two-dozen supermajority requirements currently in the state constitution," by Jason Mercier, Washington Policy Center, March 1, 2013

"Reducing Washington's 'long ballot' for elections, time to restructure statewide elected policy offices," by Jason Mercier, Policy Notes, Washington Policy Center, August 2008

CHAPTER SEVEN
CREATING JOBS AND PROTECTING WORKER RIGHTS

1. Policy Recommendation: Protect worker rights by making Washington a right-to-work state

The principle of right-to-work is simple. It is the legal right of a person to hold a job without having to pay mandatory dues or fees to a union. It does not outlaw unions; it ensures that union membership is voluntary in order to protect every worker's basic right to employment and freedom of association.

Worker rights gaining prominence

Right-to-work laws are gaining prominence across the country as state leaders strive to improve job creation, promote economic development and attract new businesses. Five states recently passed right-to-work laws. These are Indiana, Kentucky, Michigan, Wisconsin and West Virginia. In all, 27 states now protect basic worker rights, with more states introducing legislation and debating the issue every year.[1] Washington state does not currently have a right-to-work law.

Further, the U.S. Supreme Court ruled in Janus v. AFSCME that state and local employees cannot be fired or otherwise punished if they choose not to join a union. The ruling means right-to-work

---

[1] "Right-to-work resources," Labor and Employment, National Conference of State Legislatures, accessed September 25, 2019, at http://www.ncsl.org/research/labor-and-employment/right-to-work-laws-and-bills.aspx. States with right-to-work laws are Alabama, Arizona, Arkansas, Florida, Georgia, Idaho, Indiana, Iowa, Kansas, Kentucky, Louisiana, Michigan (private/public), Mississippi, Nebraska, Nevada, North Carolina, North Dakota, Oklahoma, South Carolina, South Dakota, Tennessee, Texas, Utah, Virginia, West Virginia, Wisconsin and Wyoming.

is the law for all public-sector workers, although this right is often unfairly restricted, as discussed in the next section.

Right-to-work is not anti-union

A right-to-work law does not prevent employees from joining a labor union. Labor unions operate in right-to-work states. Right-to-work laws do not force unions to represent "free riders" who take advantage of union representation but do not pay dues. Rather, right-to-work laws require unions to give workers a choice about financially supporting those efforts.

Right-to-work laws promote business and jobs

Studies show that states with right-to-work laws attract more new business than states without such laws. Right-to-work states consistently outperform non-right-to-work states in employment growth, population growth, in-migration and personal income growth. Adjusted for cost-of-living, workers in right-to-work states enjoy higher real disposable income than workers in non-right-to-work states.[2]

A 2015 economic study measured the business and employment effects if Washington became a right-to-work state.[3] The findings are dramatic. Like other right-to-work states, Washington would benefit from a permanent boost in employment and income growth.

---

2 "Right-to-work laws: The economic evidence," by Jeffrey A. Eisenach, Ph.D., Insight in Economics, NERA Economic Consulting, May 2018, at https://www.nera.com/content/dam/nera/publications/2018/PUB_Right_to_Work_Laws_0518_web.pdf, and "Real Earnings Higher in Right to Work States," Stan Greer, Senior Research Associate, National Institute for Labor Relations, January 1, 2001, at, www.nilrr.org/2001/01/01/ real-earnings-higher-right-work-states/.
3 "Impact of right-to-work on the state of Washington," by Eric Fruits, Ph.D., Policy Brief, Washington Policy Center, June 2015, at www.washingtonpolicy. org/library/docLib/Shannon-_fruits_study.pdf.

What is more, these benefits would come with no cost to the state. In fact, the study estimated the state would likely enjoy greater tax revenue from the increased economic growth:[4]

- Increased employment – After five years, the state would have almost 120,000 more people working as a right-to-work state, with more than 13,100 in increased manufacturing employment, than it would have without a right-to-work law;

- Increased incomes – After five years, the state's wage and salary incomes would be $11.1 billion higher, and average annual wage and salary would be more than $560 higher.

Right-to-work promotes fairness

The fairness inherent in right-to-work laws is clear. Worker rights advocates say workers should have the freedom to decide whether they want to support a union financially. If workers find union membership is worthwhile, they will voluntarily pay union dues. If they do not believe the benefits are worthwhile, or if they disagree with the politics and campaign spending of the union, they should not be forced to support it.

Similarly, the economic arguments supporting a right-to-work law in Washington are simple. As more states increase their competitiveness by adopting right-to-work laws, Washington's non-right-to-work status increasingly hampers the state's business climate.

Conclusion

When comparing state business climates, Washington enjoys high marks for not having an income tax, for access to world markets and for an educated, innovative workforce. Adding a right-to-work law to protect private-sector workers would serve the public interest because it would enhance Washington's economic

---

4 Ibid.

Small Business

competitiveness and promote fairness and social justice for workers.

2. Policy Recommendation: Make it as easy for public-sector workers to leave a union as it is to join one

In June 2018 the U.S. Supreme Court ruled that public-sector workers cannot be forced to join a union as a condition of employment. In *Janus v. AFSCME,* the Court affirmed the freedom of association rights of all state, county and local government employees freely to join or refuse to join a union, without penalty, harassment or loss of employment.[5]

Imposing barriers to worker rights

In April 2019, however, the Washington state legislature passed a bill, HB 1575, imposing a series of barriers on public-sector workers who wish to exercise their Janus rights. The bill passed along party lines, with only Democrats voting for it and Republicans opposing it. Governor Inslee signed the bill into law on April 30th.[6]

The new law imposes many restrictions on public-sector workers:

- Allows unions to sign up a worker based on electronic or

5 *Janus v. American Federation of State, County and Municipal Employees (AFSCME)*, No. 16-1466, Supreme Court of the United States, decided June 27, 2018, at https://www.supremecourt.gov/opinions/17pdf/16-1466_2b3j.pdf.
6 HB 1575, "Strengthening the rights of workers through collective bargaining by addressing authorizations and revocations, certifications, and the authority to deduct and accept union dues and fees," Washington state legislature, introduced January 24, 2019 by Rep. Monica Jurado Stonier (D-Vancouver), enacted April 30, 2019. at https://www.washingtonvotes.org/Legislation. aspx?ID=184135.

recorded voice message –clear written permission from the worker is no longer required;

- Requires any worker who wishes to leave the union to submit the request in writing;

- Forbids employers from recognizing a worker's Janus rights without first getting approval from the union;

- Ends ballot secrecy protections when workers vote on whether to be represented by a union. Instead, workers must sign or reject a public "show of interest" card in person in the presence of union organizers;

- Weakens safeguards against forcing union representation at a government agency, cutting the approval threshold from 70% of workers to only 50%. Combined with ending ballot secrecy in union elections, the provision allows unions to pressure workers who wish to exercise their Janus rights and not join.

A number of proposed amendments designed to restore ballot secrecy and allow workers, not union executives, to decide for themselves whether to pay dues failed along party lines.

Clear purpose is to protect the powerful

The clear purpose of HB 1575 is to protect the powerful status of unions within government agencies and to make it difficult for public-sector workers to exercise their Janus rights. In return, unions play an influential role at election time, providing financial support to candidates who promise to protect the union's privileged position.

The new law also makes it easier for public-sector unions to collect dues from unwilling employees, and to pressure workers against speaking out.

Small Business

Anti-Janus rights bill is likely unconstitutional

Since it represents a clear violation of freedom of association, HB 1575 is almost certainly unconstitutional. This point was raised during committee debate in the state House.[7] Rep. Drew Stokesbary (R-Auburn) noted the bill makes it,

"...incredibly more difficult to opt-out [of a union] than it is to opt-in," and that it exposes the state to liability for wrongful withholding of employee wages.

Democrats asserted the legislature does not have to be concerned about the constitutionality of proposed bills, saying,

"It is not in our purview to make those decisions," and that the legislature "is not the venue where we determine constitutionality, it happens across the parking lot [at the state supreme court]."[8]

Conclusion

Lawmakers should repeal the HB 1575 law and enact safeguards that protect the rights of workers in the public sector at all levels of government. State leaders should make sure that it is as easy to leave a union as it is to join one, and that all public employees are informed of their right to leave a union whenever they wish, without threats, harassment or job loss.

---

7 Hearing on HB 1575, "Collective Bargaining/Dues," Rep. Drew Stokesbary (R-Auburn), House Appropriations Committee, Washington state House of Representatives, March 11, 2019.
8 Hearing on HB 1575, "Collective Bargaining/Dues," Rep. Timm Ormsby, (D-Spokane), House Appropriations Committee, Washington state House of Representatives, TVW, February 26, 2019, at https://www.dropbox.com/s/a9sin5ywg1wvdjj/1575%20Debate.mp4?dl=0.

3. Policy recommendation: End the Service Employees International Union (SEIU) dues skim to stop unions from taking money from monthly Medicaid payments

Home health care workers are hired by disabled Medicaid recipients or their legal guardians to provide in-home personal care services. The hired worker is often a family member caring for an elderly parent or disabled child.

The Medicaid program provides a modest monthly payment, administered through the state, which allows elderly and disabled people to live in their own homes, providing a loving and cost-saving alternative to going to a nursing home or a state institution.

Union skims money from monthly checks

Thousands of disabled Medicaid recipients are unaware, however, that the SEIU union has made a special arrangement with the state to take part of their monthly Medicaid check. SEIU says it takes the money as "dues" to pay for union representation, even though many people do not know the state has labeled these home care workers as "union members."

The arrangement is highly profitable for the union. Every year SEIU skims a staggering $27 million from the Medicaid care payments sent to our state's in-home care providers.[9]

Labeling home care workers "state employees"

SEIU executives say they take the money because family caregivers are supposedly "state employees." What they do not

9 Form LM-2 Labor Organization Report, filed March 30, 2017, available at http://optouttoday.com/sites/default/files/SEIU-775-2016_LM-2.pdf.

mention is home caregivers are classified by the state as "state employees" only to collect dues, and for no other reason.

This is a legal fiction. Caregivers for Medicaid recipients are clearly not state employees. They are not hired, fired or even supervised by state managers. They do not receive the generous pay, vacation, retirement and health benefits that real state employees get.

But they must pay union dues to SEIU if they want to work as a caregiver, even to care for a member of their own family.

SEIU does not even have to do the collecting. A state agency automatically takes the money from the caregivers' Medicaid payment and gives it to the union. Home caregivers never even see the money before it is diverted to SEIU.

Union dues skim invalidated by the courts

In 2014, the U.S. Supreme Court invalidated the SEIU's Medicaid dues skim. The Court ruled that home care workers cannot be forced to pay union dues or fees against their will. To further protect the rights of the elderly and disabled, the U.S. Department of Health and Human announced in 2019 that states could not take part of monthly Medicaid payments in order to financially benefit of a third party, such as a union.[10]

Not surprisingly, SEIU executives were not happy with the Court's ruling. Since then the union has aggressively worked to prevent workers from exercising their right not to pay union dues.

---

10 "Feds officially end SEIU dues skim of Medicaid funds," by Erin Shannon, Washington Policy Center, May 2, 2019, at https://www.washingtonpolicy.org/ publications/detail/feds-officially-end-the-seiu-dues-skim-of-medicaid-funds.

Blocking homecare worker rights

SEIU has sent confusing information to caregivers, filed hostile lawsuits and even sponsored a misleading (and widely criticized) ballot initiative in 2016 to keep home care providers from being informed.[11]

In addition to those tactics, SEIU skirted the U.S. Supreme Court ruling by imposing an "opt-out" system that puts the burden of stopping dues collection on the caregivers, not on the union. Worse, the union has made the "opt-out" system as confusing and difficult as possible, saying caregivers can only leave the union during one 15-day period each year.

Conclusion

Medicaid dollars are supposed to enable the elderly, sick children, and the disabled to receive loving in-home care rather than go to a nursing home or a state institution. Instead, much of this caring support is being siphoned away to enrich a private union.

Lawmakers should end the SEIU dues skim in Washington state, see that home care worker rights are respected, and ensure they receive the full monthly Medicaid payment to which they are entitled.

Small Business

4. Policy recommendation: End secret union negotiations by subjecting collective bargaining to the Open Public Meetings Act

Washington state has one of the strongest open government laws in the country. The state's Public Records Act and the Open Meetings Act (OPMA) require that both laws be "liberally

---

11 Initiative 1501, Washington state, passed November 8, 2016.

construed" to promote open government and accountability to the public. The law says:

> "The people of this state do not yield their sovereignty to the agencies which serve them. The people, in delegating authority, do not give their public servants the right to decide what is good for the people to know and what is not good for them to know. The people insist on remaining informed so that they may retain control over the instruments they have created."[12]

Billions of dollars in public spending negotiated in secret

Despite this strong mandate for government transparency, government collective bargaining contracts in Washington are usually negotiated in secret. There is no option for the public to know what transpires in such negotiations until well after those negotiations have been concluded and agreements have been signed.

These secret negotiations between government unions and public officials often involve billions of dollars in public money.

Public shut out of talks

In practice, this means the public does not have access to the details of any contract negotiations between government officials and union executives until after an agreement has been struck. At that point, the final contract and its cost are posted on the website of the state Office of Financial Management. Even then, the details of the proposals and ensuing negotiations that led to the collective bargaining agreement are kept secret.

In order to learn exactly what a government union asked for,

---

12 Revised Code of Washington, Title 42, Chapter 42.30, Section 010, Open Public Meetings Act, at http://app.leg.wa.gov/rcw/default.aspx?cite=42.30.

what the governor or local officials gave up, one must wait until the contract is signed then file a public records request.

It typically takes two to three months to get the records. That is not an open, nor timely, means by which taxpayers, union members, lawmakers, and the media can learn what was negotiated before a contract agreement was reached.

Public employees have a right to know

It is not just taxpayers who are deprived of their right to know. Rank and file public employees on whose behalf the union negotiates are also left in the dark.

Public employees are taxpayers as well, and they may be concerned about the financial obligations public officials are committing the public to pay, especially when such obligations are agreed to in secret.

Only the government officials and union executives who negotiated the deal know what offers were made, and rejected, in collective bargaining negotiations. Public employees and the public are left wondering whether, and how well, their interests were represented.

Open collective bargaining is common in other states

Secrecy is not the rule in every state. Washington's neighbors to the south and east, Oregon and Idaho, require collective bargaining negotiations to be open to the public. Of the 47 states that allow government workers to collectively bargain, 22 states allow some level of public access to these negotiations,

In addition, seven local governments in Washington have recently ended secrecy and embraced transparency. A policy of open collective bargaining has been adopted by Gig Harbor, Ferry County, Lincoln County, Kittitas County, Spokane County and Pullman School District and Kennewick School District.

Voters in the City of Spokane are deciding in November 2019 whether to adopt a similar policy of collective bargaining openness in their community.

Conclusion

Negotiations with powerful public-sector unions should not be negotiated in secret. The public should be allowed to follow the process and hold government officials accountable for the spending decisions they make on taxpayers' behalf.

Opening public employee collective bargaining is clearly working in many states, and even in some Washington local governments, creating a more open, honest, and accountable government. Lawmakers should adopt the same policy of transparency and public openness for the state, for counties and for local-level government.

5. Policy recommendation: Legalize private workers' compensation insurance

Washington is one of only four states that bar business owners from buying affordable workers' compensation insurance in the competitive market. Only Ohio, North Dakota, Washington and Wyoming enforce monopoly systems.[13] In 46 states, employers have the ability to choose among many competing private insurers, to get the best coverage for their workers at the best price.

---

13 Workers' compensation laws – state by state comparison," Legal compliance, workers' compensation, National Federation of Independent Business (NFIB), June 7, 2017, at https://www.nfib.com/content/legal-compliance/legal/workers-compensation-laws-state-by-state-comparison-57181/.

Outlawing competition

In contrast, Washington state runs its own insurance company and sets its own prices. Buying the product is mandatory, and state officials have passed a law to make sure they face no competition. Measured in private-sector terms, the state-run insurance company is highly profitable and guarantees long-term and lucrative employment for its executives and staff.

As a result, the system is one of the most expensive in the nation. Increasing insurance choices through legal competition would help make workers' compensation more effective and less expensive.

Private insurance would increase worker safety

Legalizing private insurance would help reduce workplace injuries. Employers know a dangerous work environment and slow rehabilitation for injured workers is expensive. Private insurance companies in other states have created extensive safety training programs designed to reduce accidents and protect workers. By working closely with employers, insurance companies have dramatically reduced the risk of workplace injuries.

For example, in 2006, lawmakers in West Virginia ended a state-run monopoly and legalized private workers' compensation insurance. As a result, the cost of work-related injuries fell an average of 27 percent, saving employers about $150 million a year. Even as costs declined, injured workers received more protections and better service. The West Virginia market comprises over 270 insurance carriers, and since the year private coverage was legalized aggregate loss costs have dropped by 75%.[14]

14 Workers' compensation," Offices of the Insurance Commissioner, West Virginia, accessed September 26, 2019, at https://www.wvinsurance.gov/Workers-Compensation.

State insurance monopoly offers no choice

By running its own insurance monopoly, Washington lags behind other states. Real-world experience shows that allowing competition reduces workers' compensation costs and improves safety.

Currently, state managers know their insurance program can never go out of business. Rates go up, and workplace injuries may increase, but buying state-sponsored coverage is the law, and employers have no other choice.

Conclusion

Legalizing market competition would reduce the number of accidents and help workers who are injured return to work sooner. As the vast majority of states have found, private coverage reduces costs, increases safety and protects workers.

In a system of private choice, the state could maintain a safety-net program by being the "insurer of last resort" for firms that, for whatever reason, cannot get private worker protection coverage.

Additional resources

"Right-to-Work: What it is and how it works," by Erin Shannon, Policy Brief, Washington Policy Center, December 2014

"Impact of Right-to-Work on Washington state," by Eric Fruits, Ph.D., Policy Brief, Washington Policy Center, June 2015

"End the union's skim of home health care wages," by Erin Shannon, Policy Brief, Washington Policy Center, October 2017

"Local governments can improve transparency and accountability by opening secret collect bargaining sessions to the public," by Jason Mercier, Policy Brief, Washington Policy Center, August 2017

"Six common myths about the minimum wage," by Erin Shannon, Policy Brief, Washington Policy Center, December 2017.

"Transparency in public employee collective bargaining: How Washington compares to other states," by Erin Shannon, Policy Brief, Washington Policy Center, December 2018

"How to leave your union – everything you need to know about the Janus right-to-work decision," by Erin Shannon, Washington Policy Center, June 1, 2018

"2019 Legislative Session: Unions – 2; workers – 0," by Erin Shannon, Washington Policy Center, May 1, 2019

Small Business

CHAPTER EIGHT
EXPANDING BUSINESS OPPORTUNITIES AND EMPLOYMENT

1. Policy Recommendation: Help family businesses by repealing the death tax on estates

In 1981, Washington voters approved Initiative 402 to repeal the state estate tax. The popular measure passed by more than a two-to-one margin.[1] The initiative authorized the state to collect a "pick-up" tax based on the federal estate tax so that families paid two estate taxes.

In 2001 Congress repealed the federal estate tax, which ended Washington's "pick-up" tax as well.[2] Washington continued to collect the estate tax until the state supreme court ruled the practice illegal in February 2005.[3]

In May 2005, however, state lawmakers passed a law that both repealed the voter-approved Initiative 402 law and overturned the state supreme court ruling, and instead imposed a stand-alone Washington estate tax. The stand-alone law survived a ballot initiative challenge in 2006, leaving the legislature's estate tax in place.[4] That means that Washington is the only state that does not have an income tax but does impose a death tax on estates.

---

1 "Initiative Measure No. 402, Shall inheritance and gift taxes be abolished...?" Initiatives to the People, Elections and Voting, Office of the Secretary of State, Washington State, November 1981, accessed May 23, 2016, at https://www.sos.wa.gov/elections/initiatives/statistics_initiatives.aspx.
2 "H.R. 1836," enacted at Public Law 107-16, passed May 2001 to phase out the federal estate tax by 2010.
3 *Hemphill et al v. State of Washington*, No. 74974-4, Supreme Court of Washington, February 3, 2005, at https://caselaw.findlaw.com/wa-supreme-court/1077314.html.
4 Initiative 920, "Washington estate tax repeal," defeated November 2006.

The rate at which lawmakers impose the tax on a family with an estate varies between 10 percent and 20 percent, depending on the size of the estate. Washington's maximum tax rate is the highest of any state in the nation.[5] Families are taxed if an estate's assessed value exceeds $2.193 million, with the threshold adjusted annually, usually upward, based on inflation.[6] Family farms are exempt, but there is no exemption for family-owned small businesses.

Most states do not impose an estate tax

The policy of imposing an estate tax is becoming increasingly rare. Only 12 states and the District of Columbia impose one, and lawmakers in four states have recently repealed their estate taxes: Indiana in 2013, Tennessee in 2016, Delaware in 2017 and New Jersey in 2018.[7]

Leaders in these states recognize that the estate tax is unfair because it imposes a second tax after death on earnings that have already been taxed during a person's lifetime. It also puts a state at a competitive disadvantage compared to neighboring jurisdictions.

Estate tax falls hardest on small businesses

In passing the 2005 estate tax, lawmakers imposed a significant tax burden on Washington citizens. The state Department of Revenue collected more than $203 million in estate taxes in

---

5 "Does your state have an estate or inheritance tax?" by Morgan Scarboro, State taxes, Tax Foundation, April 5, 2018, at https://taxfoundation.org/state-estate-tax-inheritance-tax-2018/.

6 "Filing threshold and exclusion amounts, 2019," Estate tax tables, Table W – Computation of Washington Estate Tax, state Department of Revenue, at https://dor.wa.gov/find-taxes-rates/other-taxes/estate-tax-tables.

7 "Does your state have an estate or inheritance tax?" by Morgan Scarboro, State taxes, Tax Foundation, April 5, 2018, at https://taxfoundation.org/state-estate-tax-inheritance-tax-2018/.

---

the fiscal year 2018.[8] This special tax falls hardest on small businesses. Corporations do not pay the tax, and corporate ownership of a business can change at any time without incurring the estate tax.

State officials, however, make families that own small businesses pay an extra tax when ownership is passed from one generation to the next, putting these families at an unfair disadvantage compared to their corporate competitors.

Tax targets family-owned businesses

The state's estate tax suppresses entrepreneurship, impedes economic growth and discourages family businesses from remaining in or relocating to Washington. Studies consistently show that estate taxes are among the most harmful to a state's economic growth.[9] This outcome is supported by the Tax Foundation, which finds:

"Studies routinely find that estate taxes discourage entrepreneurship and lead to large tax compliance costs."[10]

Estate taxes are unfair and inefficient. Grieving families note that, after a working lifetime of paying property, sales, business and other taxes, state officials are taxing their loved one again after death. Most importantly, the tax is seen as unfair because state

Labor

8 "Estate Tax, Total," Net state tax collections by tax and fund, Table 5, Department of Revenue Collections, fiscal years 2017 and 2018, at https://dor. wa.gov/sites/default/files/legacy/docs/reports/2018/Tax-Statistics_2018/Table5. pdf.
9 "State death tax is a killer," by Stephen Moore and Joel Griffith, Backgrounder #3021, The Heritage Foundation, July 21, 2015, at www.heritage. org/research/reports/2015/07/state-death-tax-is-a-killer.
10 "Estate and gift taxes," State taxes, The Tax Foundation, accessed October 9, 2019, at https://taxfoundation.org/individual-and-consumption-taxes/estate-and-gift-taxes/.

lawmakers target family-owned businesses that can least afford to pay it, while their larger, corporate counterparts are exempt.

Conclusion

Lawmakers should repeal the outdated death tax on estates to bring greater equity and fairness to the tax code and to align Washington's tax policy on the same competitive basis like most other states.

2. Policy recommendation: Policymakers should avoid the six common myths about the minimum wage

Some public officials like to promote increases in the state-imposed minimum wage because it makes them feel generous. They are able to "give" workers a raise without having to pay for it or take responsibility for the harm that it does to young workers, the unskilled, immigrants and the unemployed.

In promoting this political message, public figures often invoke six common myths about a high state minimum wage.

Myth #1. The purchasing power of the minimum wage has not kept up with inflation

False. The Washington state minimum wage has more than kept pace with inflation.

When it started, in 1961, the state minimum wage was $1.15

an hour. In 2019 it is $12.00 an hour.[11] Adjusted for inflation, the 1961 minimum wage today would be $9.90, meaning Washington's minimum wage now is 20 percent higher than the rise in inflation over the same period.[12]

Myth #2. Minimum wage workers are worse off today than in the past

False. Today federal income tax rates for low-wage earners are about half of what they were in the past. This is due in part to tax cuts enacted under Presidents Ronald Reagan, George W. Bush and Donald Trump, and due to increases in the Earned Income Tax Credit (EITC).[13] Low-income workers can receive up to a 45 percent EITC credit, meaning they pay no income tax and often receive a cash payment from the government.

Further, the greatest tax burden on low-income workers in Washington state is imposed by state and local elected officials in the form of regressive sales taxes, property taxes and special levies. Reducing the high state and local tax burden would do more for workers than increasing the minimum wage.[14]

11 "History of Washington minimum wage, 1961 – 2019," Wage and hour rules, Washington state Department of Labor and Industries, accessed September 26, 2019, at https://www.lni.wa.gov/WorkplaceRights/Wages/Minimum/History/default.asp. In some jurisdictions, like Seattle, the minimum is $15.00 an hour, with certain exceptions. The state minimum wage is scheduled to rise to $13.50 an hour on January 1, 2020.
12 "CPI Inflation Calculator, 1961 – 2019," Bureau of Labor Statistics, U.S. Department of Labor, accessed September 26, 2019, at https://data.bls.gov/cgi-bin/cpicalc.pl?cost1=1.15&year1=196101&year2=201908.
13 "Reducing poverty via minimum wages, alternatives," by David Neumark, Federal Reserve Bank of San Francisco Economic Letter, December 28, 2015, at www.frbsf.org/economic-research/publications/economic-letter/2015/december/reducing-poverty-via-minimum-wages-tax-credit/.
14 See for example "Revenue forecast shows it is time for a sales tax cut," by Jason Mercier, Washington Policy Center, October 1, 2018, at https://www.washingtonpolicy.org/publications/detail/revenue-forecast-shows-its-time-for-a-sales-tax-cut.

Labor

Myth #3. Increasing the minimum wage will "lift workers out of poverty"

Some politicians say the minimum rate is "a starvation wage" and that people are working hard but "...going nowhere in a hurry."[15]

This is not true. Low wages are not the cause of poverty. The primary cause of poverty is the lack of a job. Of working-age adults living in poverty, nearly two-thirds do not work. Of those who do work, only 10 percent work full time. Increasing the minimum wage kills job opportunities for low-skilled, low-income people, making it more likely they will live in poverty.[16]

Myth #4. The average minimum wage worker is 35 years old

False. Data from the Bureau of Labor Statistics finds that "minimum wage workers tend to be young."[17] Only 2.7 percent of hourly workers make the minimum wage, and half of minimum wage workers are under age 25.[18]

---

15 "It's time for a national $15 minimum wage," by Senator Bernie Sanders and Senator Patty Murray, *The Seattle Times*, April 28, 2017, at www.seattletimes.com/opinion/bernie-sanders-and-patty-murray-its-time-for-national-15-minimum-wage/

16 "The effects of minimum wage on employment," by David Neumark, Federal Reserve Bank of San Francisco Economic Letter, December 21, 2015, at www.frbsf.org/economic-research/publications/economic-letter/2015/december/effects-of-minimum-wage-on-employment/, and "UW study finds Seattle's minimum wage is reducing jobs," by Janet I. Tu, *The Seattle Times*, June 26, 2017, at www.seattletimes.com/business/uw-study-finds-seattles-minimum-wage-is-costing-jobs.

17 "Characteristics of minimum wage workers," Bureau of Labor Statistics, U.S. Department of Labor, April 2017, at www.bls.gov/opub/reports/minimum-wage/2016/home.html.

18 Ibid.

Myth #5. Most minimum wage workers are supporting a family

False. Research shows most minimum wage workers are young, work part-time, have never been married, and live at home. Most minimum wage earners provide the second or third income in a household making more than $50,000 a year.[19]

Myth #6. Minimum wage has not kept up with productivity

Irrelevant. Measuring minimum wage policy against national productivity is meaningless.

Total productivity includes the value created by workers in high-tech, computer programmers, software engineers, skilled aerospace workers, highly-educated business executives and trained professionals like teachers, doctors and lawyers. Meanwhile, the minimum wage sector comprises less than three percent of the labor force, mostly representing beginning workers who quickly move up in productivity, and wage income, as they gain experience.

The level of national productivity has no relation to what wages should be for low-skill and starter jobs.

Conclusion

Many of the arguments that public figures make in pushing for a high minimum wage are not true. The state-imposed minimum wage is a price control. It sets the rate below which a worker cannot be hired so that thousands of entry-level jobs are eliminated. The result is that many workers are artificially

19 "The Effects of a $12 Federal Minimum Wage." Dr. William E. Even, Miami University, and Dr. David Macpherson, Trinity University, for Employment Policies Institute, March 2016, at www.minimumwage.com/wp-content/uploads/2016/07/MinimumWage101_PolicyBrief_July.pdf.

priced out of the labor market because the law sets their effective minimum wage at zero.

Lawmakers should be aware of how the wage mandate harms young, low-skill and immigrant workers because a high minimum wage stifles job opportunities and increases youth unemployment.

3. Policy recommendation: Allow a youth training wage

The overwhelming majority of economic studies show that a high minimum wage has the greatest negative effect on people with low-skills, such as teen workers entering the workforce. This principle is conceded by state policymakers, who already allow a starter training wage for very young workers, as described below.

Increasing barriers to employment

In 2016, voters passed Initiative 1433 to increase the state minimum wage to $13.50 by 2020.[20] That may seem like great news for the state's minimum wage earners, but the initiative increases barriers to employment. It is doing particular harm to young, inexperienced and unskilled workers who typically try to get entry-level jobs that pay the minimum wage.

The risk of hiring young workers

Hiring a 16-year-old who has no work history or marketable skills is a gamble for an employer. When the minimum wage is low, it is a risk many employers are happy to take. The lower wage

---

20 "Initiative Measure No. 1433, Concerning Labor Standards," ballot measures, Washington Secretary of State, passed November 8, 2016, at https://results.vote.wa.gov/results/20161108/State-Measures-Initiative-Measure-No-1433-concerns-labor-standards.html.

justifies the extra work employers must put in to teach a 16-year-old how to be a productive employee.

As young people gain work experience, they generally earn a raise, or move on to a higher-paying job. They also learn core character lessons that lead to lifetime success, such as how to be on time, how to have a positive attitude, how to follow directions, how to take initiative, how to be part of a team and how take pride in shared accomplishments in the workplace.

Shutting out young workers

When the minimum wage is too high, such on-the-job training becomes too expensive for employers. Many business owners stop hiring young workers, favoring applicants with more experience and proven skills instead.[21]

This is not just an opinion. Economic research shows a high minimum wage has the greatest negative effect on people with low skills, such as teen workers trying to enter the workforce. Seattle, for example, would have 5,000 more jobs available, mostly for youth, if it did not impose a high minimum wage.[22]

A University of Washington researcher studying Seattle's $15 minimum wage law explains:

"…If they [employers] are going to be paying as much as they

Labor

---

21 "U.W. study finds Seattle's minimum wage is costing jobs," by Janet I. Tu, *The Seattle Times*, June 26, 2017, at https://www.seattletimes.com/business/uw-study-finds-seattles-minimum-wage-is-costing-jobs/.
22 Ibid.

have to pay they are not taking a chance on a teenager, they are looking for a more experienced worker to fill that job."[23]

Washington lawmakers have increased the minimum wage to one of the highest in the nation. Since then, Washington has consistently ranked among the states with the highest youth unemployment.

Today, the state unemployment rate for teen workers is 20 percent, over five times higher than the general unemployment rate of 3.5 percent.[24] It is obvious that high mandated wages kill jobs for youth.

The best remedy is to allow a starter wage that is lower than the costly minimum, to counteract the job-killing effect of the Washington minimum wage law on youth employment. Research shows that lowering the minimum wage for young workers can help them find work.

The law already allows a limited training wage

State lawmakers already recognize the value of a training wage for very young workers. The strict wage mandate is eased for young people below age 16 so that employers can hire 14- and 15-year-old workers at 85 percent of the minimum wage. Officials

---

23 "Report on the impact of Seattle's minimum wage ordinance on wages, workers, jobs, and establishments through 2015," by Jacob Vigdor et al., The Seattle Minimum Wage Study Team, University of Washington, July 2016, at https://www.documentcloud.org/documents/2997999-Seattle-Minimum-Wage-Final-Report.html, and "Sawant, U.W. researchers clash over impact of $15 minimum-wage law," by Daniel Beekman, *The Seattle Times*, September 21, 2016, https://www.seattletimes.com/seattle-news/politics/sawant-uw-researchers-clash-over-impact-of-15-minimum-wage-law/.

24 "Youth unemployment rate, figures by state – Washington," Data, Economy and Finance, Governing.com, based on U.S. Bureau of Labor Statistics data, accessed October 10, 2019, at https://www.governing.com/gov-data/economy-finance/youth-employment-unemployment-rate-data-by-state.html.

---

understand that almost no one will hire a 14- or 15-year old at the high wage rate required by the state.

But the same barrier extends to hiring 16- and 17-year-old workers with no skills or experience; the high wage mandate ensures their earnings are zero because these unskilled workers can't get hired in the first place.

Legislation is not needed to ease hiring restrictions

The state Department of Labor and Industries has the regulatory authority to expand the benefits of a training wage to all workers under age 18; no new legislation is required.

Failing this, however, lawmakers should pass a bill to the same effect. Such bills have been introduced in the past, and serve as models for action lawmakers can take to increase job openings for youth.[25]

Conclusion

Policymakers should legalize a training wage for teen workers. Easing hiring restrictions would provide employers with an incentive to take a chance and hire young, unskilled and inexperienced job seekers. Such a policy would reduce the harm the state's high minimum wage has on blocking job opportunities, especially for young people.

Labor

---

25 See for example SB 6471, "Creating a teen summer employment wage," sponsored by Senator Michael Baumgartner, introduced January 28, 2014, Washington state legislature, at https://apps.leg.wa.gov/billsummary/?BillNumb er=6471&Year=2013&Initiative=false.

4. Policy Recommendation: Reduce the regulatory burden by requiring legislative oversight of agency rulemaking

Washington is one of the most heavily regulated states in the nation. A study by the Pacific Research Institute ranks Washington as the 8th most regulated state.[26] Another study, by the Mercatus Center at George Mason University, using different measures, ranks Washington as the 13th most regulated.[27] Both rankings demonstrate a regulatory environment in urgent need of reform.

Washington's harsh regulatory burden

Business owners agree. They increasingly identify Washington's harsh regulatory burden as the major obstacle to business growth and job creation.

Even state agencies acknowledge the regulatory problem in Washington. In recent years the Department of Commerce, the State Auditor, the Department of Revenue and the Washington Economic Development Commission (WEDC) have issued reports describing the morass of regulations employers must know, understand and obey in order to do business legally in our state.

Each of these agencies recommends that state officials provide regulatory relief in order to retain and attract businesses. In a strongly worded condemnation of our state's regulatory climate, commissioners at the WEDC concluded:

---

26 "The 50-State Small Business Regulation Index," by Wayne Winegarden, Ph.D., Pacific Research Institute, July 2015 at www.pacificresearch.org/leadmin/images/Studies_2015/SmBusinessIndex_UpdatedVersion2_web.pdf.
27 "Freedom in the 50 States; An Index of Economic Freedom," by William P. Ruger and Jason Sorens, Mercatus Center at George Mason University, 2013 edition, at http:// freedominthe50states.org/about.

"Washington's overly burdensome regulatory system must be addressed as a top economic development priority."[28]

15,000 pages of new rules

State agencies have replaced the legislature as the primary vehicle for day-to-day lawmaking. Unelected agency officials increasingly use the rulemaking process to impose onerous regulations that normally would not be approved by the elected legislature. In 2017, state agencies filed 1,487 new rules that fill 15,509 pages. They adopted 1,052 of those rules, amending 2,937 sections of the Washington Administrative Code.[29]

When unelected bureaucrats create so many rules, there is significantly less public accountability, transparency and debate than when elected representatives in the legislature pass new laws.

In addition to the large volume of rules is the problem of imposing regulation without public accountability or representation. Requiring legislative approval of all regulations issued by state agencies would hold unelected officials accountable for the regulations they want to impose on citizens and would hold lawmakers accountable for supporting or opposing those regulations.

Require a roll call vote on regulations

Agency officials routinely point to legislative mandates as cover for the rules they want to impose, even when the proposed rules go far beyond what lawmakers intended. Requiring a clear roll call

28 "Driving Washington's prosperity: A strategy for job creation and competitiveness," Washington Economic Development Commission, March 2013, at www.wedaonline.org/documents/ Con2014/2013StrategicPlan.pdf. 29 "Agency rule-making activity," Office of the Code Reviser, State of Washington, Table 1, 2017, at http://leg.wa.gov/CodeReviser/Documents/ rulactiv.pdf.

vote on new rules would make lawmakers responsive to the public for the regulations they have directed agencies to implement.

Conclusion

Lawmakers should require legislative approval of agency regulations to prevent agency officials from unilaterally imposing regulations with no concern for the consequences. The result would be to increase public accountability, foster relief for hard-working citizens, and provide a much-needed check on agency rulemaking activity.

5. Policy Recommendation: Provide for the automatic repeal of outdated regulations

It is difficult to imagine the sheer bulk of state regulations that are imposed every day on the people of Washington state. State regulations fill 32 thick volumes, comprising thousands of pages and forming a stack of paper over five feet high. These rules have the force of law, and they strictly control and limit the day-to-day activities of every person in the state.

Government rules are clearly needed in an orderly society. Regulations protect public safety, promote public health, assist needy families, help the jobless, protect the civil rights of all residents and guard against consumer fraud. This need was recognized by the founders of the state, who recommended "a frequent recurrence to fundamental principles," which is "essential to the security of individual rights and the perpetuity of free government."[30]

Regulations last forever

The problem is that under the current system of governing most

---

[30]   Constitution of the State of Washington, article 1, Section 23.

state regulations are written to last forever. State rules often last far longer than their intended purpose. In fact, regulations usually outlive the state officials who created them and go on limiting people's lives long after anyone can remember why they were imposed in the first place.

Within the limits of ordered liberty, it is the right of citizens to live as they see fit, not as officials in government direct. When people in state government overstep their bounds by regulating the smallest details of lawful activities, they increase their own power by hindering the vibrant economic and social life of the community.

Review rules every five years

To solve the problem of regulations that are practically immortal, policymakers should require all agency rules and regulations to carry a sunset provision – a date on which they will automatically expire. Expiration dates could be set so that state agency rules would come up for review every five years on a regular schedule and, if still needed, would be reauthorized by the legislature.

Agency managers would notify the legislature of approaching expiration dates a year in advance, giving lawmakers time to hear from the public and to review regulations to see if they are still needed.

Conclusion

The default assumption of officials should be that reducing regulations should favor citizens, not state agencies. If the legislature does not act to continue a rule, it should expire automatically, freeing citizens to make their own decisions in an area once constricted by the government.

Rules that are really necessary and enjoy broad community support should be renewed, based on proven effectiveness and genuine public need, and should continue in force until the next review period.

6. Policy Recommendation: Cut occupational licensing rules, so people who want to work are allowed to work

Washington state requires occupational licenses for many entry-level jobs which often require hundreds, even thousands, of hours of training. These strict regulations lock people out of job opportunities, and there is bipartisan agreement that reform is necessary.

Bipartisan support for reform

Republicans have long supported cutting barriers to work opportunities, and many Democrats recognize the problem too. The Obama Administration released an excellent overview of the need for reform in 2015. The report notes:

> "Lower-income workers are less likely to be able to afford the tuition and lost wages associated with licensing's educational requirements, closing the door to many licensed jobs for them." Further, the report noted that, "in many cases, the training or experience that these immigrants acquired overseas does not count toward fulfilling the relevant licensing requirements."[31]

---

31 "Occupational Licensing: A framework for policymakers," The White House, prepared by the Department of the Treasury Office of Economic Policy, the Council of Economic Advisors, and the U.S. Department of Labor, July 2015, at https://obamawhitehouse.archives.gov/sites/default/files/docs/licensing_report_final_nonembargo.pdf.

Irrational requirements

First, many of the licensing requirements are excessive and irrational. In Washington state, a manicurist must pay for 600 hours of training to qualify for a license. A license for "hair design" requires a minimum of 1,400 hours.[32]

By way of comparison, a tattoo artist requires zero hours of training. State rules that require people who need a job to spend hundreds of hours and thousands of dollars make it more difficult for them to become self-sufficient.

Not delivering health and consumer protection

Second, research shows occupational licenses do not deliver the health and consumer protection that their backers claim. The White House report found that "Stricter licensing was associated with quality improvements in only 2 out of the 12 studies reviewed."

Additionally, the Brookings Institution noted in a 2015 study, occupational licensing has impacts that "impose net costs on society with little improvement to service quality, health, and safety."[33]

Finally, research shows that licensing boards do not enforce health and safety guidelines. The Obama Administration report points out,

"There is also evidence that many licensing boards are not diligent in monitoring licensed practitioners, which

Labor

---

32 "How to get your WA license: Graduate of a school or apprenticeship program," Washington State Department of Licensing, accessed September 2019, at https://www.dol.wa.gov/business/cosmetology/get_school.html.
33 "Reforming Occupational Licensing Policies," by Morris M. Kleiner, The Hamilton Project, Discussion Paper 2015-01, March 2015, at https://www.brookings.edu/wp-content/uploads/2016/06/THP_KleinerDiscPaper_final.pdf.

contributes to a lack of quality improvement under licensing. These boards often rely on consumer complaints and third-party reports to monitor practitioner quality."[34]

Most third-party complaints come from current, licensed workers trying to block competition from unlicensed workers. More complaints are registered with the Better Business Bureau or online with Yelp than with the state licensing board.

Legislators should take four important steps to help provide job opportunities.

Removing barriers

First, Washington should remove barriers to people with criminal records. Research from Arizona State University found:

"...government-imposed barriers to reintegration into the labor force – particularly occupational licensing requirements – can be among the most pernicious barriers faced by ex-prisoners seeking to enter the workforce."[35]

States like Illinois[36] and Tennessee adopted reforms saying that licensing boards:

---

34 "Occupational Licensing: A framework for policymakers," The White House, prepared by the Department of the Treasury Office of Economic Policy, the Council of Economic Advisors, and the U.S. Department of Labor, July 2015, at https://obamawhitehouse.archives.gov/sites/default/files/docs/licensing_report_final_nonembargo.pdf.

35 "Turning shackles into bootstraps: Why occupational licensing reform is the missing piece of criminal justice reform," Policy Report, No. 2016-01, Center for the Study of Economic Liberty at Arizona State University, by Stephen Slivinski, November 7, 2016, at https://research.wpcarey.asu.edu/economic-liberty/wp-content/uploads/2016/11/CSEL-Policy-Report-2016-01-Turning-Shackles-into-Bootstraps.pdf.

36 State of Illinois, "SB 1688 Enrolled," Concerning state government, at http://www.ilga.gov/legislation/publicacts/100/PDF/100-0286.pdf.

"...shall not deny an application for a license, certificate, or registration, or refuse to renew a license, certificate, or registration, solely or in part due to a prior criminal conviction that does not directly relate to the applicable occupation, profession, business, or trade."[37]

Currently, Washington state law says unrelated criminal convictions do not immediately disqualify a job applicant, but a past conviction for any offense may be considered in the hiring process.[38]

Second, lawmakers should significantly reduce the license requirement in many areas of work. Requirements for many occupations do not reflect the risk of the job and are instead used by incumbents to lock out competition. This is true of many cosmetology licenses, where hour requirements could be replaced with a test of safety and health knowledge.

Hourly requirements could be replaced by an online portal with independent consumer ratings. Such a system would be more public and would more effectively publicize questions about health and safety than the existing system.

Third, require regular review of occupational licenses. Nebraska recently adopted legislation that required "present, significant, and substantiated harms" that warrant government intervention, and that legislators must first consider a regulation that is the "least restrictive" and imposes the lowest burdens and costs while still protecting consumers from the harm.[39] The law also has a "sunset

Labor

37 State of Tennessee, "Senate Bill 2465," To amend the Tennessee code, at http://www.capitol.tn.gov/Bills/110/Bill/SB2465.pdf.
38 Revised Code of Washington 9.96A.020, "Employment, occupational licensing by public entity – prior felony conviction no disqualification – exemptions," at https://app.leg.wa.gov/RCW/default.aspx?cite=9.96A.020.
39 "Nebraska Governor signs landmark reform for occupational licensing," by Nick Sibilla, Press Release, Institute for Justice, April 23, 2018, at https://ij.org/press-release/nebraska-governor-signs-landmark-reform-occupational-licensing/.

review" where legislative standing committees examine one-fifth of the state's occupational regulations to identify any rules or laws that should be repealed or modified.

Finally, Washington state should recognize occupational licenses from other states. Military families, migrants and others who relocate should not be required to start over when they have already demonstrated knowledge and skill in performing a particular job. Arizona recently passed legislation recognizing out-of-state licenses for those with at least one year of experience.[40]

Conclusion

Occupational licenses are intended to promote public health and safety. They should not be used as a mean-spirited barrier to deny work to immigrants, criminal offenders, and workers seeking to gain new skills. Washington should reform and reduce these barriers, to give people the opportunity to earn the dignity and happiness that comes with self-sufficiency and earned success.

---

40 State of Arizona, "House Bill 2569," Relating to occupational licensing, 2019, https://www.azleg.gov/legtext/54leg/1R/bills/HB2569H.pdf.

Additional resources

"Why I hate and love the free market," by Jim Boulanger, President, Patriot Fire Protection, Inc., Policy Notes, Washington Policy Center, January 2019

"Six common myths about the minimum wage," by Erin Shannon, Policy Brief, Washington Policy Center, December 2017

"Cities are starting to see the harsh reality of high minimum wage laws," by Erin Shannon, Policy Notes, Washington Policy Center, December 2017

"This editorial should be required reading for every policymaker," by Erin Shannon, Washington Policy Center, May 1, 2017

"Remove obstacles to the American dream, including absurd professional licensing laws," by Todd Myers, Washington Policy Center, guest op-ed in *The Seattle Times*, March 27, 2017

"Reducing the burden of the death tax on families," by Jason Mercier, Legislative Memo, Washington Policy Center, December 2016

"SB 6396 would bring review and accountability to agency rule-making," by Erin Shannon, Legislative Memo, Washington Policy Center, February 2016

Labor

CHAPTER NINE
IMPROVING MOBILITY AND
TRANSPORTATION SERVICES

1. Policy Recommendation: Direct public spending to traffic congestion relief and increasing mobility rather than reducing trips

Providing traffic congestion relief is the most basic tenet in transportation policy, yet state officials do not actually tie annual spending to measurable benchmarks of progress that would require them to improve mobility and reduce people's commute times.

In 2000, Washington's Blue Ribbon Commission on Transportation identified several ways to measure the effectiveness of the state's transportation system. These performance measures were very specific, and some were adopted into law. They included:

- Traffic congestion on urban state highways shall be significantly reduced and be no worse than the national mean.

- Delay per driver shall be significantly reduced and no worse than the national mean.

Lawmakers repealed benchmarks

However, in 2007, lawmakers repealed those benchmarks and replaced them with five vague transportation policy goals. Lawmakers added a sixth goal in 2010. Only one of the six policy goals sought to reduce travel times. "Mobility," as the legislature defines it, is an effort to "improve the predictable movement of goods and people throughout Washington State," not necessarily improve travel times.

Lawmakers enhanced the policy goal of better mobility as part of the 2015 transportation package by adding Washington Policy Center recommendations to improve congestion relief and speed freight mobility, but they decided against continuing the performance-based benchmarks that had previously been part of the law.

The continued lack of performance benchmarks is based on the Washington State Department of Transportation (WSDOT) Secretary's pessimistic view that "Traffic congestion…is a problem we simply cannot solve."[1]

Failing to report traffic delays

WSDOT officials have even stopped reporting statewide delay altogether, despite being required by statute to reduce traffic congestion. The agency is, instead, focused on reducing vehicle trips, managing congestion through tolls, and encouraging transit expansion and use. This policy of reducing rather than accommodating people's daily trips, promoted by broad moral and environmental claims about vehicle pollution, is counterproductive to a growing and healthy economy.

Rather than spending billions of dollars on alternatives most working families will not use, any pollution or access-related problems with automobiles should be solved head-on (for example, by making automobiles cleaner, and by allowing safe deployment of automated vehicles to enhance mobility for low-income, disabled and senior communities).

---

1 "WSDOT's Roger Millar: 'We must become stewards of the transportation system,'" American Association of State Highway and Transportation Officials (AASHTO) Journal, July 20, 2018, at https://news.transportation.org/Pages/072018millar.aspx#.W1XWL6CGBNA.twitter.

Reducing traffic congestion by 20 percent

The Washington State Auditor's office determined in 2007 that over a five-year period, if congestion relief were prioritized, it could be reduced up to 20 percent, lowering vehicle emissions and saving travelers up to $400 million.[2] The Auditor's Office said that transportation spending "should be measured, in part, based on how many hours of delay can be reduced for each million dollars" spent.[3]

The Auditor also recommended lawmakers, "Apply congestion-related goals, objectives and benchmarks to all highway and transit-related investments" and "elevate congestion reduction benefits in all decision-making processes."[4]

Conclusion

Lawmakers should amend current transportation law to return to a system based on performance metrics like those identified by Governor Locke's Blue Ribbon Commission. Reinstating these measures would show the public that policymakers are committed to reducing traffic congestion and making trips quicker to increase mobility in ways that serve the public interest.

2. Policy Recommendation: Use more public-private partnerships to improve roads and reduce costs

Officials in Washington state say they need more money to pay for transportation infrastructure. They claim traditional funding

---

2 "Washington State Department of Transportation, Managing and Reducing Congestion in Puget Sound," Performance Audit Report, Washington State Auditor's Office, October 10, 2007, at http://portal.sao.wa.gov/ReportSearch/Home/ViewReportFile?arn=1000006&isFinding=false&sp=true#search=congestion%20relief
3 Ibid.
4 Ibid.

methods like state and federal gas taxes are not keeping up with the rising cost of Washington's transportation program, resulting in growing problems in meeting the state's transportation expansion, maintenance and safety needs.

Artificial cost increases, however, like rules that inflate prevailing wages, excessive planning, permitting mandates and the practice of state officials taxing their own construction projects, continue to put pressure on budgets to maintain and expand infrastructure. As public demand for highway travel outpaces the supply of travel lanes, drivers experience increased traffic congestion. As an example, the city of Seattle ranks sixth for worst traffic congestion in the United States, with drivers wasting 138 hours each year sitting in traffic. [5]

Tapping the private sector

In many states, officials are tapping the private sector to maintain and expand public roads and increase mobility, while reducing costs. Public-private partnerships are a popular way to build public roads both in other countries and in states like Virginia, Texas, Florida and California.

A public-private partnership is a legal contract between government officials and private companies to design, build, operate, maintain and finance needed public infrastructure. In short, public-private partnerships allow the public sector to shift financial risk from taxpayers to private investors.

Blocking innovative partnerships

In Washington, however, state officials are reluctant to use private financing to build public infrastructure. Washington was one of the first states to adopt a public-private partnership law in

5 "INRIX 2018 Global Traffic Scorecard," INRIX Analytics, Kirkland, Washington, 2018, at http://inrix.com/scorecard/#.

1993, but changing political circumstances led to the law's repeal with passage of the Transportation Innovations Partnerships Act of 2005.

The bill's title indicated intent to attract private capital for highway projects, but the text of the law has had the opposite result, effectively blocking private investment in building public infrastructure in Washington.

Officials say traffic congestion in the Puget Sound region will continue to worsen, raising costs and stifling economic growth. Congestion also harms the environment, as cars, trucks and buses idle in traffic, leading to lower air quality and increased public health risks.

Conclusion

Lawmakers should recognize the positive role private finance can play in building public infrastructure and improving mobility in our state. Amending the restrictive 2005 law would attract private investment to public projects, get badly needed road projects built, and protect taxpayers from higher taxes and bailouts.

3. Policy Recommendation: Improve Sound Transit's accountability and governance

The regional transit authority in the Puget Sound region known as Sound Transit is governed by a board of 18 appointed members, including the Secretary of the WSDOT. Fourteen of these members are local elected officials who are hand-picked by just three people: the county executives of King, Pierce, and Snohomish counties. The majority (nine) of the board member appointments are controlled by one person: the King County Executive.

Transportation

Not accountable to voters

Like any other legislative body, the Sound Transit Board meets regularly, is subject to transparency and open meeting laws, has taxing authority, and makes policy and budget decisions for the agency. Unlike a legislative body, however, the board is appointed and not directly accountable to voters.

The practice of appointing board members to a powerful public agency, especially when one person controls most appointments, shields Sound Transit officials from the direct accountability one might expect from a large, multi-billion-dollar government agency.

Weak public oversight

Sound Transit's accountability arm, the Citizen's Oversight Panel (COP), is supposed to be an independent group of citizen experts that serve a watchdog role, yet its members are hand-picked by the very officials the COP is intended to watch, the unelected Sound Transit Board of Directors. This presents a serious ethics conflict.

In 2012, the State Auditor found many conflicts of interest both within the board and its Citizen Oversight Panel, which was packed with former board members and favored individuals who worked for companies that profited from Sound Transit contracts.[6]

Violating the "one person one vote" principle

In addition, Sound Transit's federated board violates the "one person one vote" principle, because some residents have several board members representing their interests, while others may

---

6 "Sound Transit: Performance Audit of the Citizen Oversight Panel, Adjustments to Planned Investments, Construction Management and Ridership Forecasts," Washington State Auditor, October 25, 2012, at http:// portal.sao. wa.gov/ReportSearch/Home/ViewReportFile?isFinding=false&arn=1008277.

---

only have one. For example, under the Sound Transit's Board structure (as of late 2019), a West Seattle resident has three people representing his interests on Sound Transit's Board, while a resident of Mill Creek only has one.

The Washington State Auditor looked at Sound Transit's governance in 2012 and found that:

> "When citizens cast their votes for most of these city and county officials, they have no way of knowing whether or not they will one day serve on Sound Transit's Board, or the positions they may take if appointed."

> "Sound Transit voters have no say regarding who will represent them and limited recourse if they are dissatisfied with the decisions of Sound Transit's Board."[7]

Therefore, the public is unable to hold Sound Transit directly accountable for cost overruns, delayed projects and concerns over subarea equity and sweeping eminent domain decisions.

Conclusion

The state of Washington has long had a reputation for clean, honest local government. That image is put at risk when a powerful and well-funded public agency like Sound Transit is controlled by the political allies of three country executives, and when the majority of its board members are personally appointed by one elected official.

A new governance structure for Sound Transit would reduce favoritism and special interest influence, would be more democratic, and would enable citizens to have a greater voice and equal representation on the governing board.

Transportation

---

7 Ibid.

4. Policy Recommendation: Reform state toll policy to benefit drivers, rather than government agencies

In 1921, officials imposed Washington's first gas tax of one cent per gallon. With this new revenue stream, state leaders were able to build, maintain, and expand Washington's highway network. As the state's transportation infrastructure needs increased, so did the gas tax rate.

Today, Washington's gas tax rate of 49.4 cents, coupled with the federal gas tax rate of 18.4 cents, is 67.8 cents per gallon, the fourth highest in the nation.

Protecting gas tax revenue

Eighty years ago, as they often do today, politicians saw a new and stable revenue stream and began to divert gas tax collections to programs and services not related to roads and highways.

More than $10 million in gas taxes were diverted to other purposes in the 10 years between 1933 and 1943. Washington voters saw this diversion as unfair and dishonest. In 1944 they voted to add the 18th Amendment to the state constitution to fix the problem. The amendment legally protects fuel taxes and vehicle license fees deposited into the Motor Vehicle Fund, which must be used for highway purposes only.

Adding tolls to public roads

Yet as costs have increased due to wasteful policies, state transportation officials looked to tolls as both a new funding source and a way to manage travel behavior.

People intuitively support public programs and services funded through direct user fees. Road tolls are no exception. When tolls are used to pay for a piece of public infrastructure, like a bridge or a length of highway, and are removed once the project is paid off, drivers naturally understand and generally support the added temporary cost.

Similarly, when tolls are imposed to manage demand, and the revenue is spent on the highway where it was collected, users reluctantly agree to pay. For the payer, tolls fund a visible project that results in a tangible benefit.

Diverting road toll revenue

However, as Washington's early experience with gas taxes illustrates, the public becomes less supportive when officials divert toll money to benefit other user groups. People naturally see a diversion of toll revenue as unfair.

State lawmakers have authorized tolling on five highway facilities:

- Tacoma Narrows Bridge;
- State Route 167 HOT lanes;
- Interstate 405 Express Toll Lanes;
- State Route 520 floating bridge;
- State Route 99 deep-bore tunnel in Seattle.[8]

Yet only toll revenues from the Tacoma Narrows Bridge and the Interstate 405 Express Toll Lanes are sent to the Motor Vehicle Fund and are protected for highway purposes only.[9]

---

8 Lawmakers authorized tolling on the Columbia River Crossing project in 2012, but authority was cancelled on December 31, 2015 as the project was dismantled.
9 "Transportation Resource Manual," Joint Transportation Committee, Washington State Legislature, page 233, January 2015, at http://leg.wa.gov/JTC/trm/Documents/TRM_2015%20Update/CompleteTRM2015.pdf.

Officials divert the toll money taken from drivers using the State Route 520 Bridge, the State Route 167 HOT lanes, and the State Route 99 tunnel in Seattle outside the Motor Vehicle Fund and spend them on non-highway purposes.

This diverted revenue can be used for the "operation of conveyance of people or goods," suggesting toll revenue not in the Motor Vehicle Fund could be diverted to transit, a non-highway purpose.

Instead of diverting taxes and fees drivers pay to non-highway purposes like transit, officials should constitutionally protect toll revenue for highway purposes only, as is done with gas tax revenue. An even better policy would be to direct road toll revenue to the state Motor Vehicle Fund, thus making sure it is constitutionally protected.

Using tolls to manage travel behavior

In addition to being a major funding source for public officials, tolls are used by the WSDOT to manage traffic congestion (rather than reduce it) and control driver behavior.

This practice is most evident on Interstate 405, where WSDOT officials have wrongly taken existing, paid for travel lanes and imposed tolls. Officials had promised that the toll program was a temporary pilot program, dependent on performance and specific requirements.

In 2018, the toll program failed to meet state and federal requirements that the toll lanes move vehicles 45 miles per hour at least 90 percent of the time. Instead of ending tolls as promised, state officials expanded the tolls and made them permanent.

Even worse, WSDOT and lawmakers nullified the speed requirement on which future toll operation depended, by making it obsolete.[10] Further, they allowed the state to take out loans against future toll revenue, borrowing money and promising to pay it back with tolls that drivers would pay over the next few decades.

On Interstate 405 in particular, the legislation sets up a conflict between WSDOT and the traveling public they are supposed to serve. If the tolls are tied up in paying back long-term debt, WSDOT officials have to maintain gridlock in no-toll general-purpose lanes to make their costly toll lanes look attractive by comparison.

A better approach to tolling policy

Officials should reconsider this self-serving approach to tolling policy and review real alternatives that respond sincerely to public needs. Alternatives that increase travel choices for all drivers, including those who cannot afford to pay tolls every day.

Washington Policy Center recommends the following five guidelines for implementing tolls that are fair for everyone:

1. The state should have the sole authority to impose tolls unless otherwise delegated through a defined public-private partnership;

2. Tolls should only be implemented on new lane capacity or to replace an existing public facility. Converting existing, underused HOV lanes to tolled HOT lanes qualifies because it adds new capacity for single-occupant vehicles. Early tolling on an existing roadway should be prohibited since taxpayers have already paid for it. Imposing tolls on existing infrastructure should be prohibited for the same reason;

10 Senate Bill 5825, "Addressing the tolling of Interstate 405, state route number 167, and state route number 509," Washington State Legislature, 2018 Legislative Session, at https://app.leg.wa.gov/billsummary?BillNumber=5825& Year=2019&Initiative=false.

3. If the goal of pricing a roadway is to manage demand, the tolled facility must provide drivers a reliable non-tolled alternative;

4. Toll revenue should be constitutionally protected by the state's 18th amendment and reserved for highway purposes only;

5. Money from tolls should be spent only on the same road on which the tolls were collected. Only the new capacity or the replaced facility that provided the toll should benefit from the revenue. Applying tolls to a broadly defined corridor is not fair to drivers who pay the toll.

Conclusion

To earn the trust and support of the public, lawmakers should set the priority for spending toll revenue in the following order: 1) Pay off debt on new roadways; 2) Maintain an existing roadway; 3) Expand a new roadway.

5. Policy Recommendation: Reduce the cost of building roads and ferries

One of the most significant obstacles to building transportation infrastructure in Washington state is the ever-rising cost of public projects. To re-build public trust and restore accountability, lawmakers must reduce regulatory delay and lower construction costs, before they seek to increase the financial burden they impose on taxpayers.

Imposing artificial costs on public projects

In a broad sense, there are two drivers of costs in transportation projects: natural and unnatural. Natural cost drivers occur as a result of normal economics, and they apply equally to the private and public sectors. These include inflation, material expenses, market labor costs, and higher costs for new technology.

Unnatural costs are imposed by government officials when their chosen policies artificially increase expenses on public works projects. These policies are implemented for reasons that are completely unrelated to actually building a public project.

Unnatural cost drivers include prevailing wage rules, imposing taxes on state projects, apprenticeship requirements, inefficient permitting, environmental compliance, setting aside money for public art, "Build in Washington" provisions, and requiring that mass transit be included in highway projects.

A real-world model for cutting artificial costs

On May 23, 2013, the Skagit River Bridge, which carries Interstate 5, was hit by a truck and the structure collapsed. Three people suffered minor injuries, and the main road connection between Vancouver, B.C. and Seattle was severed.[11]

The Governor and all the members of the state's elected leadership rushed to replace this essential link. They eliminated the artificial policies that normally add lengthy delay and increased costs to any public project. Intense media and public interest allowed state officials to suspend normal practice and repair the road connection quickly and efficiently.

Officials had a temporary replacement bridge open in less than a month, on June 19th, and a permanent span was open to traffic by September 15, 2013. The public saw first-hand how eliminating

11 "I-5 bridge collapses over Skagit River; possibly triggered by truck," by Brian M. Rosenthal, *The Seattle Times*, May 23, 2013, at http://blogs. seattletimes.com/today/2013/05/bridge-collapses-on-interstate-5-over-skagit-river/.

Transportation

inefficient and artificial rules can get a road project completed and provide immediate mobility benefits.

Important reforms

After the collapse, the public demanded reforms to reduce unnatural costs and political delays on transportation projects. In their 2015 transportation package, lawmakers chose to keep taxes paid on highway projects in the transportation account, reducing the diversion of tax revenue.

Lawmakers also created a limited-open bidding system for ferry construction, and they worked to streamline permitting on bridge replacements.

Conclusion

The reforms were a good first step but they do not go far enough to cut artificial costs, improve service and rebuild trust with the public. Lawmakers should continue to reduce unnatural cost drivers to provide mobility and congestion relief to the public for less money.

6. Policy Recommendation: Ensure that any proposed mileage-based user fee directly benefits and protects drivers

Ease of travel and mobility, and the road construction and maintenance that it requires, is the key to economic strength and security in the modern world. People are willing to pay gas taxes and fees if they trust that officials will provide a direct mobility benefit in return. In Washington, this public-trust model has not worked, as taxpayers have been told repeatedly to pay more into a system that fails to reduce traffic congestion and improve mobility for everyone.

Proposing a new tax

The Road Usage Charge (RUC) Pilot Project in Washington is the newest funding proposal, promoted by officials as a "user fee" and "gas tax replacement."

This pilot project took place in 2018, led by the Washington State Transportation Commission (WSTC) and involved about 2,000 participants. The project was intended to test the idea of imposing a mileage tax on Washington drivers and to see whether it would be politically feasible to do so. In the experiment, volunteers received simulated invoices based on a flat charge of 2.4 cents for each mile they drove on public roads.

Drivers had five reporting options, including pre-paying for the number of miles they wished to drive, submitting mileage by taking pictures of their odometers, or installing a GPS-enabled transponder in their vehicles.

Some transportation analysts see a mileage-based user fee (also known as a miles-traveled tax) as a fair and even ideal way of paying for public roads. This method is technically feasible, and even politically feasible if the state gas tax is entirely eliminated, administrative costs are significantly lowered and privacy and security safeguards are in place.

These policy parameters, are critical because, implemented the wrong way, this tax is certain to worsen the problem public officials say they want to solve, namely the funding and maintenance of our road system.

Used for spending unrelated to roads, a RUC would not be a targeted user fee or true gas tax replacement (as asserted by the WSTC and others), but a new general mileage tax on the public. To be a user fee, the money must be directed into the Motor Vehicle

Transportation

Fund and protected by the state constitution's 18th Amendment, like the gas tax is, and used for highway purposes only.

A social policy to change people's behavior

Additionally, social policy objectives revealed by the WSTC in 2013 suggest officials would attempt to use a mileage tax to change people's driving behavior, which would be in line with current state policy that seeks to reduce per-capita driving by 50 percent by 2050.[12]

However, any reduction in driving would reduce either fuel or mileage tax revenue, meaning this state policy conflicts with the mileage tax objective of generating more revenue than the current fuel tax.

It is unlikely this policy conflict would be resolved in a way that is favorable to the public. There are only two ways a mileage tax would not undermine state driving reduction targets, which are questionable and likely unachievable, to begin with.[13] First, lawmakers could make the per-mile rate progressively higher, perhaps by indexing it to inflation and eliminating any need for future public votes on rate increases.

Second, they could impose a carbon tax to make driving less fuel-efficient cars less attractive as a means of escaping payment of a higher mileage tax (which is intended to collect dollars from the owners of more fuel-efficient vehicles). People would then be left

---

12 "Washington State Road Usage Charge Assessment: Feasibility Assessment, Work Plan, and Budget Report to the Legislature," Washington State Transportation Commission, January 23, 2013, at https://wstc. wa.gov/StudiesSurveys/RoadUsage/RUC2012/documents/2013_02_ WARoadUsageChargeAssessment.pdf.
13 Revised Code of Washington 47.01.440, "Adoption of statewide goals to reduce annual per capita vehicle miles traveled by 2050 – Department's duties – Reports to the legislature," Washington State Legislature, 2008, at https://apps. leg.wa.gov/RCW/default.aspx?cite=47.01.440.

with either paying a very high gas tax (inclusive of a carbon tax), or a very high mileage tax.

Concerns about loss of privacy and reduced mobility

The 18th amendment trust fund debate, as well as the social impact of a potential mileage tax, have controversial policy implications that could end any possibility of adopting a true mileage-based user fee. The idea will fail if people believe government officials will collect mileage tax money from drivers and then spend it in any way they want to, with little or no public accountability. Even more worrisome is the great social cost the public would pay in the form of lost personal privacy, autonomy, and mobility.

A RUC, as a policy in Washington state, is not likely to represent a true and fair user fee and should be rejected if designed as a general mileage tax.

Conclusion

If lawmakers consider a gas tax replacement in the form of a true per-mile user fee, the aforementioned policy concerns should be resolved first, and the policy should be presented to the public in the form of a referendum for voter approval, rather than imposed as a top-down legislative mandate.

7. Policy Recommendation: Ensure Washington regulations support the safe testing and use of automated control in cars, buses and trucks

The development of automated transportation, including personal vehicles and new forms of transit, are changing the transportation landscape. Automated transportation, which allows some or all driving functions to be performed by the vehicle, has the potential to increase safety, efficiency, access, and mobility for everyone.

Automated driver assistance in vehicles is now going beyond anti-lock braking systems (ABS) and electronic stability control to adding new features like automatic lane-keeping ability and adaptive cruise control. These innovations are already reducing accidents and speeding up traffic.

Automation also creates a market opportunity for people to simply buy the rides they need rather than a buying car. According to experts, "both [ride-share and car buying markets] will be significant, mutually competitive, and demanding of space, infrastructure, regulation, and investment."[14] Thus, whether people buy trips or cars, "the total economic position of the automotive industry will strengthen."[15]

Need for updated regulations

While there are still many unknowns, the "advent of highly automated vehicle may require modernization of our motor vehicle codes, auto safety regulations, infrastructure investment, products liability law, and location transportation service regulations" to help people adapt to this new way of looking at mobility."[16]

In June 2017, Governor Jay Inslee issued Executive Order 17-02, which established the state's first Autonomous Vehicle Work Group to advance the Governor's objective of "enabling safe testing and operation of autonomous vehicles on public roadways,"

---

14 "The End of Driving: Transportation Systems and Public Policy Planning for Autonomous Vehicles," by Bern Grush and John Niles, Elsevier press, 2018, page 74.

15 Ibid.

16 "Self-Driving Regulation, Pro-Market Policies Key to Automated Vehicle Innovation," by Marc Scribner, On Point No. 192, Competitive Enterprise Institute, April 23, 2014, at https://cei.org/sites/default/files/Marc%20 Scribner%20-%20Self-Driving%20Regulation.pdf.

---

the benefits of which include the reduction of collisions caused by human error, improving mobility for those who are elderly or disabled, and "maximizing our ability to move people and goods quickly and safely throughout the state."[17]

In 2018, Governor Inslee signed Substitute House Bill 2970, which required the WSTC to "convene a work group to develop policy recommendations to address the operation of AVs on public roadways in the state."[18]

Washington Policy Center is a working member of the work group's subcommittee on infrastructure and systems, focusing on roadway infrastructure, traffic management, transit service and vehicles, advertising, right of way, multi-modal transportation and mobility as a service (MaaS).[19]

New rules should not be too restrictive

Through the AV Work Group and this subcommittee, officials at the WSDOT and volunteer members are working to finalize a policy framework for "cooperative automated transportation" in our state. While this is a meaningful exercise, many of the policy goals that have been drafted are either unnecessary or too prescriptive at such an early stage.

---

17 "Autonomous Vehicle Testing and Technology in Washington State and Autonomous Vehicle Work Group," Executive Order 17-02, Governor Jay Inslee, Washington, June 2017, at http://governor.wa.gov/sites/default/files/exe_order/17-02AutonomouVehicles.pdf?utm_medium=email&utm_source=govdelivery.
18 "SHB 2970, Establishing an autonomous vehicle work group," Final Bill Report, Washington State Legislature, June 7, 2018, at http://lawfilesext.leg.wa.gov/biennium/2017-18/Pdf/Bill%20Reports/House/2970-S%20HBR%20FBR%2018.pdf.
19 "Infrastructure and Systems Subcommittee," Washington State Transportation Commission, at https://wstc.wa.gov/Meetings/AVAgenda/Documents/InfrastructureSystemsSubcommittee.htm.

Transportation

An example would be the draft policy specifying that "particular emphasis should be given to buttress effective and convenient high capacity public transit," and that automated transportation should "not compete with it." Another example would be that the policy should empower "local partners to achieve their economic vitality and livability goals" and "meet the needs of traditionally marginalized communities."[20]

To facilitate the safe testing and deployment of automated transportation in our state, it is critical that laws and regulatory systems do not impose restrictions that "narrow the scope of permissible development" or unnecessarily delay adoption, thereby increasing costs to the public.[21]

Protecting the traveling public

At the same time, roads are used by the general public in a variety of ways, and reasonable steps to maintain public safety are warranted.

For example, policymakers should maintain the rules for illuminating cars at night with functioning headlights and taillights, even as technology is being deployed to make that lighting more effective. Some of the state responsibility for protecting the public on public roads will be carried out as a result of the state synchronizing its motor vehicle code with other jurisdictions to reflect new technology applications. This should be done through

---

20 "Cooperative Automated Transportation (CAT) Draft Policy Framework – Working Document," by Ted Bailey and Daniela Bremmer, Washington State Department of Transportation, November 26, 2018, at https://www.wsdot. wa.gov/sites/default/files/2019/01/22/Cooperative-Automated-Transportation-Policy-Framework-for-AASHTO-20181126.pdf.

21 "Self-Driving Regulation, Pro-Market Policies Key to Automated Vehicle Innovation," by Marc Scribner, On Point No. 192, Competitive Enterprise Institute, April 23, 2014, at https://cei.org/sites/default/files/Marc%20 Scribner%20-%20Self-Driving%20Regulation.pdf.

national professional interaction based on agreement among the states.

WSDOT should focus on a concise set of policies that are useful and practical today, working closely with national efforts from well-established public interest and professional groups such as the National Council of State Legislatures, the American Association of Motor Vehicle Administrators, and the Governors Highway Safety Association (GHSA).

Legislators should eliminate regulations that are too restrictive and confusing, and pass new laws if experience shows they are needed to protect the public.

Conclusion – advancing personal freedom

The vision for automated transportation and personal mobility must be neutral as to travel mode, focused on the advancement of personal freedom, choice and movement across all available travel choices, and include public transportation, cars, light trucks, electric and human-powered bicycles and motorcycles.

Government management of the public right of way should protect public safety while recognizing the importance of car and truck mobility in supporting the economic life of the region. Prioritizing policies that support agency and infrastructure readiness would commit officials to actionable policies, and would be the best approach.

Transportation

Additional resources:

"I-405 toll lanes are not working, alternatives should be considered, by Mariya Frost, Policy Brief," Washington Policy Center, April 2018

"WSDOT demonstrates that adding general purpose capacity on I-405 reduces traffic congestion and toll rates," by Mariya Frost, Washington Policy Center, July 14, 2017

"The Road Usage Charge: To impose a tax on every mile you drive," by Mariya Frost, Policy Brief, Washington Policy Center, June 2017

"Voters should elect Sound Transit board members directly," by Mariya Frost, Policy Notes, Washington Policy Center, August 2016

"Five Principles of Responsible Transportation Policy," by Bob Pishue, Policy Brief, March 2015

"Ending 'Build in Washington' rule would cut ferry construction by 30%," by Bob Pishue, Legislative Memo, Washington Policy Center, March 2015

"How to reduce the cost of highway projects," by Bob Pishue, Legislative Memo, Washington Policy Center, February 2014

CHAPTER TEN
IMPROVING AGRICULTURE

1. Policy Recommendation: Protect the H-2A jobs program

Washington agriculture faces a growing labor need to maintain its place as a leader in food production. A key element in filling farm jobs is a robust migrant labor force, which in turn provides opportunity and income for migrant families.

As farmers and ranchers in Washington continue to compete for access in the global marketplace, they must have employees to help grow and harvest their crops.

The federal H-2A work program

An important part of creating farm jobs is the federal government's H-2A work visa program. Authorized by Congress, the program permits workers from Mexico and other countries to work legally on farms in the United States.

The H-2A program provides jobs, income and access to housing and health care for migrant workers. It also encourages stability and community growth, as workers develop a relationship with employers, reducing the need for migrants to move around the country at harvest time.

Benefits to Washington state

The H-2A work program provides significant benefits to the public interest in Washington state. In 2016, there were approximately 97,000 seasonal farmworkers employed in

Washington.[1] In the same year, 13,689 H-2A temporary agricultural work visas were approved for Washington employers.[2]

H-2A temporary agricultural work visa

The size and popularity of the H-2A temporary agricultural work visa program highlight the need for additional agricultural labor. The use of the H-2A visa program is an expensive, time-consuming and last-resort process for employers in Washington and, yet, it is often used to the maximum extent possible each year. According to the U.S. State Department, participation in the H-2A visa program grew by 218 percent between 2007 and 2017, more than doubling the size of the program.[3]

Conclusion

Critics of H-2A work visas say farmers and ranchers are "exploiting" workers by providing good-paying jobs. However, the program is entirely voluntary and is popular with employers and workers. The H-2A jobs program is over-subscribed, with far more migrant workers seeking visas than places available each year.

Because it serves the public interest and contributes to food security, lawmakers should protect the H-2A jobs program from needless state-imposed costs. The state should not place added fees and restrictions on this federal program and should work for its expansion so that migrants can get jobs legally in the state.

---

1 "Farmworker services," Jobs and Training, Washington State Employment Security Department, accessed November 12, 2019, at https://esd.wa.gov/jobs-and-training/farmworker-services.

2 "Office of Foreign Labor Certification Annual Report 2016," Employment and Training Administration, U.S. Department of Labor, https://www.foreignlaborcert.doleta.gov/pdf/OFLC_Annual_Report_FY2016.pdf.

3 "Unlimited cheap farm labor: Evaluating H-2A disclosure data," by Preston Huennekens, Center for Immigration Studies, August 6, 2018, at https://cis.org/Report/Unlimited-Cheap-Farm-Labor-Evaluating-H2A-Disclosure-Data.

---

2. Policy Recommendation: Enhance labor force training in agriculture to promote jobs and increase food production

Despite automation and the use of modern machinery, food production is labor intensive, requiring trained and dedicated workers to manage the land, bring in harvests and feed the world.

The Food and Agriculture Organization of the United Nations projects a world population of 9.1 billion by 2050.[4] The demand a population of that size places on the food system will require labor to help with the cultivation and harvesting of those crops.

Policy shift away from manual labor

In the early 2000s, there was a shift in educational discussions away from trades, vocations and manual labor to promote traditional four-year college for everyone, with the heavy implication that manual blue-collar jobs are undignified.

As a result, policymakers have focused education and training policies on fast-growing sectors of high-tech communications, computer software and aerospace, while neglecting the labor needs of the rural areas of the state.

The blue-collar labor force has aged and rural communities find it difficult to attract new employees. Today, the agricultural sector is experiencing a labor gap, making it harder to harvest crops and maintain the food supply.

---

4 "Global agriculture towards 2050, How to feed the world 2050," High Level Expert Forum, Food and Agriculture Organization 2050, Rome, October 12 - 13, 2009, at http://www.fao.org/fileadmin/templates/wsfs/docs/Issues_papers/ HLEF2050_Global_Agriculture.pdf.

Agriculture

The dignity of manual work

Far from being seen as undesirable or not respectable, manual labor enhances human dignity and service to the community. The public policy discussion of education and development needs to shift back to an emphasis on the dignity of manual trades, vocations and the essential value of blue-collar jobs.

The way to promote that dignity is to emphasize the potential to build a better life through human-development programs like FFA and 4-H.[5] These programs encourage entrepreneurial initiative, engineering skills, and mechanically-minded abilities for the betterment of agriculture that can be put to use on the farm.[6]

Alternative educational and training opportunities

The first step to solving labor needs for Washington farmers and ranchers is to promote the development of the agriculture-sector workforce. This is best done by offering a wide range of alternative education and training options.

Career and Technical Education (CTE) programs, Skills Centers, technical colleges, apprenticeships and similar programs match students with their interests and abilities. These learning programs provide educational alternatives to traditional four-year programs, which often do not serve the life-skill needs of students and tend to burden them with long-term debt.[7]

---

5 Future Farmers of America and 4-H; Head, Heart, Hands and Health.
6 "Celebrating career and technical education," by Cyndie Shearing, FFA New Horizons, Future Farmers of America, February 15, 2018, at https://www.ffa. org/ffa-new-horizons/celebrating-career-and-technical-education/.
7 "Skill Centers, Career and Technical Training," Office of the Superintendent of Public Instruction, Washington state, accessed October 30, 2019, at https:// www.k12.wa.us/student-success/career-technical-education/skill-centers.

Conclusion

Policymakers should devote equal attention and resources to educational alternatives and vocational training in the agricultural sector. This approach would open new job opportunities in the domestic workforce and help to fill the labor needs of farmers and ranchers in Washington state.

3. Policy Recommendation: Protect job opportunities and overtime exemptions for farm workers

A 40-hour work week is standard for city-based jobs but does not fit the needs of many agricultural employers. State law provides important exemptions in cases when government-imposed work rules don't make sense.[8] From the beginning, lawmakers have protected rural jobs by providing an overtime exemption for farm workers. Those exemptions are now at risk.

Exemption is based on the nature of farm work

The policy exists for good reason. The cyclical nature of farm work makes the agricultural exemption essential to successful harvests and in promoting food security in Washington state.

Over 300 food items are grown and raised in Washington. Periods of planting, growing and harvesting are seasonal and highly weather-dependent, and farm labor needs vary accordingly.

For example, early spring planting and late summer to early fall harvests throughout most of Eastern Washington require long hours in the fields. Other periods, during winter and mid-summer, are slower. To offset the long hours required at certain times, most

---

8 Revised Code of Washington 49.46.130, "Minimum rate of compensation for employment in excess of forty hour workweek – exceptions," accessed November 12, 2019, at https://apps.leg.wa.gov/rcw/default.aspx?cite=49.46.130.

farmers and ranchers shorten workdays for employees whenever possible.

Flexible scheduling

Flexible scheduling is essential to rural life. Entire families pitch in at harvest time, while slow seasons are a chance for a more relaxed work pace, county fairs and community activities. The need for flexibility is reflected in the yearly school schedule, which still preserves the rhythm of country life.

The overtime exemption for farm employees gives farmers a way to effectively run their businesses without pricing them out of the employment market. The exemption also gives farm employers the ability to exercise discretion in how they compensate their employees for their hard work.

Salaried wage structure

To preserve job opportunities, some farmers and ranchers are providing workers with a regular salary structure, meaning workers can rely on a steady income regardless of seasonal variations in work hours.

By providing employees with a steady rate of pay, regardless of hours, farmers are able to reduce turnover and build a team of good workers who have institutional knowledge of operations on a particular farm.

In doing so, farmers and ranchers are adopting a hiring practice that is common among city-based employers. Some activists say farm workers should not be paid with a fixed salary, but they rarely question a computer programmer working a variable schedule of 50 hours one week and 10 the next while being paid the same fixed salary every week.

Providing employment security

The key advantage of flexible scheduling and regular salaries for farm workers is that it avoids seasonal layoffs. Farmers and ranchers want to retain good employees, and they have every incentive to protect workers from the intermittent nature of agricultural work.

This finding is supported by the example of a worker earning $15 an hour on an occasional basis who is laid off during slow times. Such a jobless worker might be eligible to receive around $1,552 a month in unemployment benefits.

However, if that same worker earns $15 an hour on a salaried basis, he can earn a steady $2,400 a month regardless of how many hours are worked, with the added benefit of employment security.

Respecting the dignity of work

It is misleading, though, for policymakers to focus simply on hours and dollars. Equally important is the need to respect the dignity of work and the job choices of workers.

State lawmakers should not impose their own arbitrary roadblocks to undo the voluntary and mutually beneficial decisions of farmers and workers. When state officials make certain work hours illegal, they shut down access to job opportunities, and deny workers the personal worth and independence that comes with earning a living.

Conclusion

Lawmakers should respect rural communities and avoid imposing arbitrary city-style work rules on farm and ranch workers. Lawmakers may think they are punishing employers,

Agriculture

but repealing the overtime exemption would fall hardest on workers because they would become subject to layoffs, lost job opportunities and be denied the dignity of earning an income.

4. Policy Recommendation: Remove gray wolves from the Endangered Species list

Just over a decade ago, there were no wild gray wolves in Washington state. Now, the population is thriving, as anticipated under the targets set by the state for recovery. Contrary to popular belief, gray wolves were not officially re-introduced to Washington state. Rather, a successful breeding pair was discovered in 2008, marking the first such pair seen in the state since the 1930s. The natural, wild wolf population then grew quickly.

Successful population recovery

A decade later, the Washington Department of Fish and Wildlife reports there are 126 gray wolves in 27 packs throughout the state, most of them located in the Northeastern part of the state.[9]

This meets the scientific standard set by the Department of Fish and Wildlife Gray Wolf Conservation and Management Plan for a "recovered species." According to state officials, the scientific recovery standard for the wild wolf population in Washington is 15 breeding pairs for three years.[10] The current self-sustaining wolf population meets that level.

---

9 "Gray wolf conservation and management," Species and Habitats, Washington Department of Fish and Wildlife, accessed November 12, 2019, at https://wdfw. wa.gov/species-habitats/at-risk/species-recovery/gray-wolf.

10 Gray wolf conservation and management plan," Species and Habitats, Washington Department of Fish and Wildlife, accessed November 12, 2019, at https://wdfw.wa.gov/species-habitats/at-risk/species-recovery/gray-wolf/management-plan.

Unrealistic state plan

State officials, in part, responding to political pressure groups, say that a healthy wild wolf population is not enough. They assert that wild wolf packs must be distributed throughout the state.

Yet tracking data shows the area in which wild wolves are thriving, Northeast Washington, provides the perfect gray wolf habitat: Easy access to denning sites; rugged terrain with few people; broad ranges and valleys for roaming packs; and access to abundant natural food sources.

These ideal conditions indicate that expecting easy dispersal of wolf packs beyond the bounds of Northeast Washington is not realistic or supported by the science.

Protecting lives and property

Gray wolves are wild predatory animals. They hunt in packs and will target any creature that is too small, weak or sick to escape or fight back. Ranchers need to be able to protect livestock, which are not part of a wolf pack's natural prey, from depredation.

Coexistence with apex predators that have returned to an ecosystem relatively recently involves competing needs, but a healthy balance can be achieved if all parties are willing to come to an agreement.

Conclusion

Since the wolf population has recovered and is in a healthy, self-sustaining state in the wild, the gray wolf should be de-listed from the Endangered Species Act. This would reduce conflict and demonstrate to the public that the Act is successful in helping a natural species recover.

Agriculture

The Colville Indian Tribe, for example, allows tribal hunters to kill wolves year-round. The tribal government also removed the three-wolf limit, indicating the thriving state of the wild population.[11]

To maintain wolf populations and reduce conflict with ranchers, a post-recovery plan should be developed with the local knowledge of ranchers most affected by depredation. Potential policies include increasing compensation payments when wolves kill livestock and more support for non-lethal options like range riding and similar herd protection. Washington policymakers can also learn from other states, like Montana, where wolf recovery has been managed successfully.

Ultimately, the best solution will come from people on the ground, working out solutions that manage the risks of wolf re-introduction when wild populations are rapidly increasing toward recovery goals.

5. Policy Recommendation: Maintain free trade and open access to Washington ports

Washington farmers produce food for a global market. Government agencies operate a system of modern port facilities built and maintained in part with tax money. Without public access to the state's ports, Washington's agricultural sector would shrink to a fraction of its current size.

In 2017, the state exported more than $15 billion worth of food and agricultural products to people around the world, more

---

11 "Colville Tribe removes wolf hunting limits for members," by Eli Francovich, *The Spokesman Review,* February 22, 2019, at https://www. spokesman.com/stories/2019/feb/22/colville-tribe-removes-wolf-hunting-limits-for-mem/.

than half of which was grown or raised in Washington.[12] To cite one example, Washington is a top exporter of food to Asia. Beneficiaries of Washington crops include people in Japan, China, South Korea and the Philippines.

Washington ports are the closest mainland ports to Asia, as well as providing access to global markets. Modern transport allows Washington farmers to improve nutrition and vary the diets of millions of people worldwide.

The ports of Seattle, Tacoma and Longview are major shipping points for Washington products, in addition to goods transported from other states. Further, all-weather highways and the barge system on the Columbia and Snake rivers allow swift and safe shipment of farm produce. These are public facilities, built and maintained for the purpose of allowing the people of Washington to connect with the world.

Port shutdown hurts growers

The ability of growers to move products came to an abrupt halt in 2014 and 2015 because of strikes. Union action shut down West Coast ports, resulting in millions of dollars in lost revenue for farmers and other food producers. Tons of fresh fruit and vegetables rotted in warehouses at 29 ports along the West Coast during the strike. Washington state apple growers, for example, lost an estimated $100 million.[13]

Overall, in-state businesses lost an estimated $769.5 million

12 "Washington is the third largest exporter of food and agricultural products in the U.S.," Export Statistics, Washington State Department of Agriculture, accessed October 30, 2019, at https://agr.wa.gov/departments/business-and-marketing-support/international/statistics.
13 "Washington farmers dump millions of apples after ports dispute," NBC News, May 29, 2015, at http://www.nbcnews.com/news/us-news/washington-farmers-dump-millions-apples-after-ports-dispute-n366426.

Agriculture

during the port shutdown.[14] Not included in this estimate is the loss of global market share for Washington growers, which may take years for them to recover.

The port slowdown dragged on for many months without action by state or federal officials to intervene, as they had done in previous port disputes.[15] The controversy had nothing to do with the private market. It occurred at facilities built and operated by government agencies. The lack of action by public officials caused even greater financial loss for Washington's farm families and businesses.

Conclusion

As a matter of policy, state lawmakers and federal officials should ensure the public has regular and dependable access to Washington ports and that these public facilities are protected from unions and damaging labor disputes.

Further, a policy of open exchange and free trade should be a priority for state and federal policymakers, to ensure that Washington growers can reach markets around the world. The public interest of Washington's agricultural communities should not suffer because of the narrow economic agenda of organized labor or any other special interest.

---

14 "The economic costs of the 2014-2015 port slowdown on Washington state, Community Attributes, Inc., Washington Council on International Trade, February 2016, Exhibit 3, page 9, at http://wcit.org/wp-content/uploads/2011/08/WCIT-Port-Delays-Economic-Impacts-Report-FINAL1.pdf.

15 "Is president considering 'nuclear option' in ports dispute?," by Elizabeth Weise, *USA Today*, February 18, 2015, http://www.usatoday.com/story/news/2015/02/18/labor-secretary-perez-west-coast-ports-ilwu-dispute/23611117/.

Additional resources

"Tough times call for open markets," by Pam Lewison, Washington Policy Center, June 5, 2019

"Senate's H-2A bill builds a wall of unnecessary paperwork," by Pam Lewison, Washington Policy Center, March 13, 2019

"HB 1398 would add costs and reduce work opportunities for legal migrant workers," by Pam Lewison, Legislative Memo, Washington Policy Center, February 2019

"Gray wolf management highlighted by H.B. 1045," by Pam Lewison, Washington Policy Center, January 17, 2019

"How U.S. trade disputes affect Washington state's agricultural communities," by Madi Clark, Policy Brief, Washington Policy Center, January 2019

"How Washington farmers would benefit from reforms to the federal Farm Bill," by Madi Clark, Policy Brief, Washington Policy Center, July 2018

"Farmers meet diverse demands, including keeping food affordable," by Madi Clark, Policy Brief, Washington Policy Center, April 2018

"Free trade a boon to workers, the environment," by Todd Myers, Washington Policy Center, guest op-ed in *The Spokesman-Review*, November 12, 2017

"Agriculture: The cornerstone of Washington's economy," by Chris Cargill, Policy Brief, Washington Policy Center, March 2016

THE POLICY EXPERTS
ABOUT THE EDITOR AND AUTHORS

PAUL GUPPY | Vice President for Research

Paul Guppy is a graduate of Seattle University and holds Masters degrees in public policy and political science from Claremont Graduate University and The London School of Economics. He served for 12 years in Washington D.C., mostly as a Legislative Director and Chief of Staff in the United States Congress, before joining Washington Policy Center in 1998 as Vice President for Research. He is the author of numerous studies on economics, government regulations, budget and tax policy, labor policy, health care, education and other issues. He is a frequent commentator on radio and TV news programs, online, and in newspapers across the state.

CHRIS CARGILL | Eastern Washington Director

Chris Cargill graduated from Gonzaga University with a B.A. in broadcast communication studies and political science. Before joining WPC, he worked in television news for ten years at the FOX and ABC affiliates in Spokane. He has served on a number of community boards, including the Spokane Valley and Tri-City Regional Chambers, as well as the Spokane Regional Transportation Commission. He is the author of numerous policy studies on Eastern Washington issues and is a frequent guest host and commentator on news radio stations throughout the state.

Liv Finne is a graduate of Wellesley College and of Boston University School of Law. She retired from civil litigation practice to raise two children and work with her husband in running a small business. She is the author of the study *An Option for Learning: An Assessment of Student Achievement in Charter Public Schools*, which in 2012 helped lead to passage of Washington's voter-approved charter school law state. She also wrote *Washington Policy Center's Education Reform Plan: Eight Practical Ways to Improve Public Schools*. She is the author of WPC's  widely-read online education blog, and a frequent commentator on public education choice and school reform in news media across the state.

Mariya Frost was born in Russia, immigrated to the United States with her family in 1993, and grew up in Washington state. She is a graduate of the University of Washington with a degree in Political Science and has completed courses in accounting and business administration at Saint Martin's University. She spent ten years working in the private sector and as a staff member at the U.S. House of Representatives and the Washington state senate. She is on the Board of Directors for the Eastside Transportation  Association, a member of the Jim MacIsaac Research Committee, the Washington State Autonomous Vehicle Work Group, and the Women of Washington civic group. She is a widely-recognized expert in state transportation policy; her analysis and online commentary appear regularly in news coverage statewide.

PAM LEWISON | Director, Initiative on Agriculture

Pam Lewison is a graduate of Washington State University. She worked eight years as a journalist in Washington, Idaho, and Oregon before earning a Master of Science in Agricultural Leadership, Education, and Communications from Texas A&M University. She has worked with the East Columbia Basin Irrigation District and as the Communications Director for the Washington Cattlemen's Association. She has also volunteered to advance agricultural knowledge through youth development programs with the Cattle Producers of Washington and Grant County 4-H program. She and her husband are farmers, raising hay, wheat, corn, and beans in the Columbia Basin. Her commentary on agricultural issues has been featured in the news, opinion columns, and radio interviews throughout the Northwest.

JASON MERCIER | Director, Center for Government Reform

Jason Mercier is a graduate of Washington State University. He served on the board of the Washington Coalition for Open Government and was an advisor to the 2002 Washington State Tax Structure Committee. Jason is an ex-officio member for the Tri-City Regional Chamber of Commerce and serves on the Chamber's government affairs committee. He worked with lawmakers to create the state's renowned budget transparency website www.fiscal.wa.gov. In 2010, former Governor Gregoire appointed Jason as a member of her Fiscal Responsibility and Reform Panel. He has testified numerous times before legislative committees on government reform issues, and his commentary and op-eds appear regularly on T.V., radio and in newspapers around the state.

Todd Myers is one of the leading experts on free-market environmental policy, including two decades of experience in research and policy analysis. He served on the executive team at the Washington State Department of Natural Resources and is a member of the Puget Sound Salmon Recovery Council. He is the author of *Eco-Fads: How the Rise of Trendy Environmentalism Is Harming the Environment*, and his work has appeared in *National Review, The Wall Street Journal* and *USA Today*. He is a beekeeper and holds a master's degree from the University of Washington.

Dr. Roger Stark is a retired cardiac surgeon and a graduate of the University of Nebraska's College of Medicine. He is the co-founder of the open heart surgery center at Overlake Hospital in Bellevue. He is the author of numerous health care studies including *The Impact of Federal Health Care Reform on Washington State* and the book *The Patient-Centered Solution*. He has testified before Congress on Medicaid, the state health insurance exchanges, and co-ops in the Affordable Care Act. His commentary and analysis has appeared in statewide and national news coverage. Dr. Stark has served on the Governing Board of Overlake Hospital and is the past Chairman of Overlake's Foundation Board.

Board of Directors

(as of 1/1/2020)

WASHINGTON
POLICY CENTER
Improving lives through market solutions

INVEST IN IDEAS
MEMBERSHIP CLUBS

**Your generous donation to WPC qualifies you for
annual membership benefits!**

WPC Member—$50 - $999
Members receive all of our research publication mailings, our quarterly Viewpoint magazine,
regular email updates and invitations to general WPC events at a discounted member rate.

Patron Member—$1,000 - $4,999
Same benefits as WPC Member and invitations to private WPC events, quarterly updates from our President and exclusive Patron lapel pin.

Benefactor Member—$5,000 - $9,999
Same benefits as Patron Member and exclusive Benefactor lapel pin, recognition in our Annual Report and private briefings from our President and Board Chairman.

President's Council Member—$10,000+
Same benefits as Benefactor Member and exclusive President's Council lapel pin, recognition at all WPC events, annual recognition in our quarterly Viewpoint magazine, insider information and regular progress reports about how your investment is making an impact, and complementary admission to WPC general events.

Pillar Society Member
Same benefits as Presidents Council Member and VIP tickets or a table at the Annual Dinner, exclusive Pillar Society name badge and invitation to private Pillar Society exclusive events, including Evening in the Desert in Palm Springs and our Summer Dinner Series.

Young Professionals Member: $100
For WPC supporters under 40 years old, same benefits as Patron Member and receive our monthly e-newsletter The INK, access to our mentorship program, invitations to our YP exclusive events and discounted or free tickets to all WPC general events.

*Washington Policy Center is a tax-exempt 501(c)(3) nonprofit organization.
To preserve our independence, we accept no government funding, and we do
not perform contract work. Contributions are deductible for federal income tax
purposes as allowed by law. Our tax-id # is 91-1752769.*

WASHINGTON
POLICY CENTER
Improving lives through market solutions

es, I am proud to support Washington Policy Center with a gift of:

❑ $50   ❑ $100   ❑ $250   ❑ $500   ❑ $1,000   ❑ Other: $ _____

ne _____

dress: _____

y: _____ State: _____ Zip _____

ail: _____

one: _____

ment Information:

☐ My check payable to *Washington Policy Center* is enclosed

☐ Please charge my:
    ❑ Visa   ❑ Mastercard   ❑ AMEX

    Name: _____

    Card Number: _____

    Exp. Date: _____ Today's Date: _____

    Signature: _____

Donate online at washingtonpolicy.org/Donate
or mail this reply card to PO Box 3643, Seattle WA 98124